Get Ready for Work

An illustrated, interactive reference guide to career planning. Taking the heat out of your job search and assisting you in moving on to a secure career.

Martin Haigh

Foreword by Lorna Aitken

Alligned to the Gatsby Benchmarks

W

Get Ready for Work

Published by Woven Word
An Imprint of Fisher King Publishing
The Studio
Arthington Lane
Pool in Wharfedale
LS21 1JZ
England

Contents

Foreword

I have the privilege of holding the position of Teacher of Technology & Business together with being Head of Information, Advice and Guidance, Continuing Professional Development and Careers Leader at Brighouse High School. During the past six years I have worked with Martin Haigh on a variety of programmes, including Super Learning Days with a focus on Careers, a range of presentations / assemblies related to Preparation for Working Life as well as our Decisions @ 18 Conference. Martin has been really supportive and has created a plethora of activities and learning materials for us. He has been our Careers Ambassador since 2015 and has provided CPD for teaching staff, to support our Careers Events.

Martin approached me and asked about the viability of this book and when he showed me the manuscript I thought that the content would be of enormous help not only to careers specialists but particularly to young people preparing for and seeking employment. Teachers involved in Careers Education want relevant, up-to-date, practical and adaptable resources to use and students need access to physical resources too. This book draws on Martin's expertise in business and provides useful strategies in an easy to read format. It has many valuable linkages not often found in careers texts and with the addition of the Gatsby Benchmarks, the cross-referencing will not only support student's career learning, but enhance careers programmes in all stages of education.

I hope you enjoy this book and I am delighted to recommend this inspirational read.

Lorna Aitken

Abstract

Focusing on your direction in life comes easy to some people and they know exactly what they want to do for a job, but for others, deciding on a career path can be one of the most daunting experiences of their lives.

This interactive book provides readers with an array of tools and ideas to help them prepare for and find interesting, stimulating employment (or self-employment). Both key skills (CV writing, job searching etc) and behavioural aspects (how to build rapport, how to conduct yourself in an interview etc) are covered and blended together in a logical pathway to success. Also included in this book is a list of useful references and links to websites established to support with your career choices.

The contents and exercises in the book are cross-referenced to the Gatsby Benchmarks so that teachers and careers specialists can use the stand-alone exercises in class and refer to the Gatsby code.

As you progress through the book please feel free to complete the many helpful exercises. However, if you do not wish to write in your book then all of the exercises and blank tables are provided free as a resource pack. Just go to www.lattitude7.co.uk to download your resources.

Acknowledgements

I am delighted that you have chosen to read this book. This publication would not have been possible without the help of Stephen Taylforth of PURO Solutions for his expert advice on formatting and Elizabeth Waterman for proofreading the entire manuscript. I would like to extend my thanks to Lorna Aitken of Brighouse High School and C&K Careers for their specialist advice and for support with the Gatsby cross-referencing. I would like to thank my wife, Melanie for her continued patience, love and understanding.

I would also like to acknowledge the organisations who have provided factual information, and for their permission to reproduce some of the images in this publication.

Finally, I am indebted to the students and graduates who have attended my training programmes and made really helpful suggestions on many aspects of their career journeys.

Martin Haigh

Introduction

Whether you are leaving school in year 11, staying on to complete 'A' or 'T' – levels, graduating from University or looking for an apprenticeship, you may feel overwhelmed by the options and, indeed the advice surrounding recruitment and career planning. This book is designed to take the heat out of your job search and help you feel positive about moving on to a secure career path.

This book is written in a modular fashion and, whilst, there is a continuous theme running through the book, the chapters are 'stand alone'. Therefore, the reader can dip in and out as every little helps. This book goes beyond career search and covers the broader topics of presenting, pitching, confidence, resilience and self-belief.

Contained in the book are specific chapters on topics such as employer needs, decision making, the mechanics of career planning and advanced interview skills including coverage of 'strengths-based' and 'competency-based' approaches. Networking skills, how to find employers, time management and how to manage stress during the job search period are also included. The content of specific chapters has been ratified by experts in the particular field.

This book is written in an easy to read style which will encourage readers to continue browsing and learning more about how to plan and secure an interesting, stimulating, sustainable job.

Good luck!

Adding Value through Gatsby

Introduction

The rapidly-changing nature of the world of work is demanding increased efforts to support young people as they make the transition from education to employment. We know that, by 2030, 85% of jobs that school leavers will be going into have not yet been invented which means that students need to be extremely well-prepared and flexible during this education-work transition. Thanks to the Gatsby Foundation there now exists a clear map of what good careers provision looks like.

The importance of delivering good career education and guidance in schools and colleges has never been greater and, from September 2018, new statutory guidance set out the requirement for every school to have a named Careers Leader. They will *lead, manage* and *co-ordinate* the school's careers programme, across all the Gatsby Benchmarks.

The Gatsby Benchmarks come out of a research project led by Professor Sir John Holman for Lord Sainsbury's Gatsby Charitable Foundation. In this project Sir John worked with researches from the International Centre for Guidance Studies at the University of Derby to explore **good** career guidance. Together they reviewed the existing research, visited numerous countries and looked at practice in independent schools and state schools in England. Out of this evidence and further consultations they came up with **eight** areas that schools, colleges and careers specialists should focus on (the Gatsby Benchmarks).

These eight benchmarks are the core dimension of good careers and enterprise provision in education, and are:

1. A stable careers programme
2. Learning from career and labour market information
3. Addressing the needs of each pupil
4. Linking curriculum learning to careers
5. Encounters with employers and employees
6. Experiences of workplaces
7. Encounters with further and higher education
8. Personal guidance

Many schools and colleges now achieve every benchmark and, The Sutton Trust research report showed that "Establishments holding the standards get better student results and less drop-out. There is also a major impact on reducing the number of NEETS (people not in education, employment or training).

How this book adds value

Given the aforementioned impact of the application of Gatsby Benchmarks we have included cross-references to the relevant Gatsby Benchmarks in all the exercises contained in the chapters. The topics in this book are highly relevant to the first four benchmarks and the book also goes some way to underpinning benchmarks five to eight.

Each section has the Gatsby Benchmark referenced so readers and teachers can immediately see the relevance. An Appendix at the end of the book explains the Gatsby Benchmark Initiative in more detail and there are also a number of references included in the Useful References section.

About You

Many young people enter the world of work without really considering what they are good at and what they are genuinely interested in. So, what is it that you are good at and what are you interested in? To make this clear, ask a friend to tell you and make sure your outside interests are clear – this can tell an employer a lot about you. To help you consider this, please take a look at the Attributes Wheel in Figure 1.

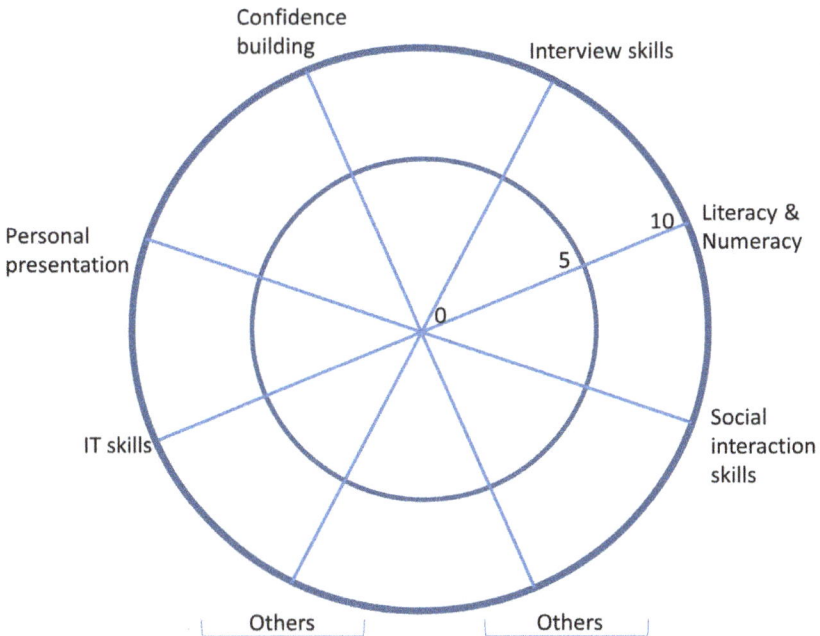

Figure 1 Attributes Wheel – blank (Gatsby 1, 4)

Now, as shown in the example in Figure 2, take the opportunity to add a couple of new categories (important to you) at the bottom of the wheel in Figure 1, then take a pencil and make a mark somewhere on each line, on a scale of 0 to 10 from the centre outwards. Now, join the marks with a straight line and this will give you a visual clue of where your current attributes are ranked. In the example given in Figure 2, personal presentation and social interaction skills are high whilst IT skills and literacy/numeracy are less well developed.

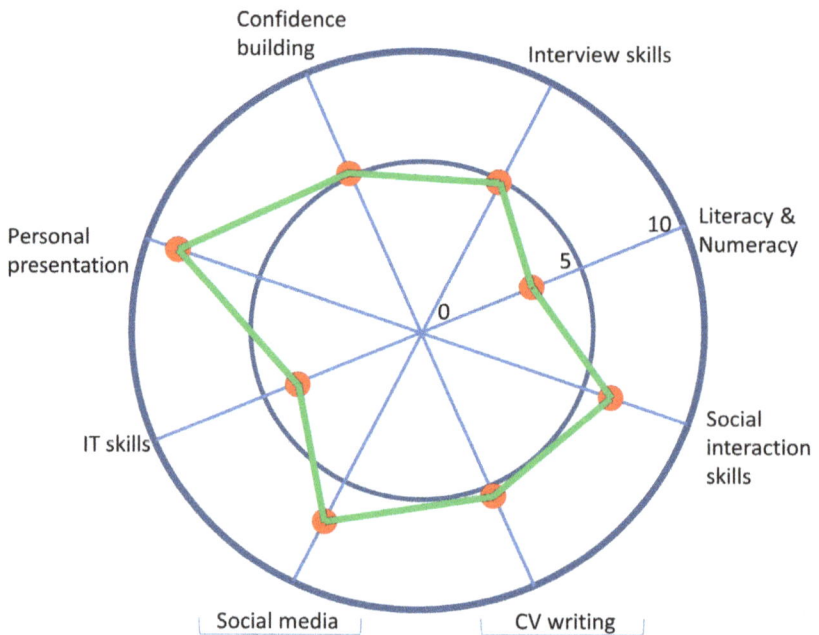

Figure 2 Attributes Wheel – example (Gatsby 1, 4)

What do you want out of a career/job?

Here is your opportunity to think about your short-term, medium-term and long-term goals.

Short-term goal examples might be: to take a junior position in, say, engineering and see if the industry is right for you.

My Short-term goals are:

Medium-term goal examples might be: to work in a role for a couple of years in order to consolidate your learning and application and, perhaps, gain experience that might contribute towards Chartership of an awarding body.

My Medium-term goals are:

Long-term goal examples might be: to have a settled career with a reputable employer and work towards an agreed career path with increasing levels of responsibility and promotional opportunities.

My Long-term goals are:

What do employers want and need?

When embarking on a career search journey, it is often useful to start with the end in mind and try to put yourself in the shoes of the employer. Take a look at the table, Figure. 3 and circle the attributes that you believe an employer might be interested to see in a job applicant.

Circle the important attributes

Creativity	Show initiative	Flexibility
Open Minded	Presentation	Soft Skills
Problem Solving	Common Sense	Hard Skills
Self Awareness	Delivery to deadlines	Take Responsibility
Working with Others	Self motivated	Networking
Communication	IT Skills	Driving/Transport
Resilience	Social Media	Positive Attitude
Financial awareness	Team working	Personable

Figure 3 Table of Employer wants and needs (Gatsby 1, 4, 5)

You can add some more attributes in the box below to make the 'employer needs' picture more comprehensive.

What can you bring to an employer?

We often underplay our strengths and overplay our development needs. Think about the Star Chart below in Figure 4 and, for the three categories, enter your strengths. The example in Figure 5 will give you an idea of how to complete the Star Chart.

Things I can do	Things I'm good at	Things I'm proud of

Figure 4 Personal Star Chart – blank (Gatsby 1, 4)

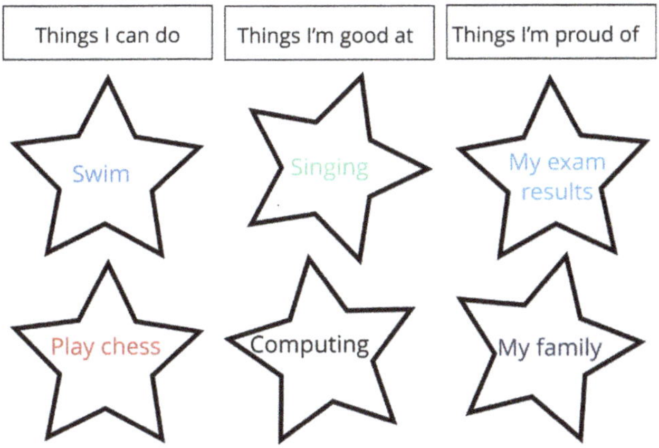

Things I can do	Things I'm good at	Things I'm proud of
Swim	Singing	My exam results
Play chess	Computing	My family

Figure 5 Personal Star Chart – example (Gatsby 1, 4)

Where are the gaps?

Now you know what employers are looking for and you are now more aware of your personal attributes, what gaps still exist that you feel you need to bridge in order to be in a strong position to secure a suitable job/career? Consider the table below, Figure No. 6, and complete this with a trusted teacher, friend or colleague. This awareness of the existing gaps but, more importantly, the actions to resolve them will help you to focus on the areas that you need to spend, perhaps, a little bit more time on.

Perceived gap	Action step to bridge the gap
Example – pitching and presenting	*Consider the points in this book or enrol on a short course on pitching skills*

Figure 6, Table of Perceived gaps and resulting actions (Gatsby 1, 4)

How to fill the gaps

Do not worry if you feel that you don't know how to fill the perceived talent/skill shortfalls, courses are available to help you fill those gaps.

Examples of available support networks are given in Figure 7 (and Figure 53) but, specifically, may include:

Topic	Support from:
Communications	National Careers Service - Provides information, advice and guidance to help you make decisions on learning, training and work. nationalcareersservice.direct.gov.uk
Interpersonal skills	National Careers Service
CV writing	CV Library - Postcode-selectable open vacancies and writing tips www.cv-library.co.uk
Job searching	Job Search - Provides job search directory - www.gov.uk/jobsearch
Pitching	National Careers Service
Interview skills	Career Cake has many resources and video tutorials on job searching www.careercake.com

Figure 7, Table of Courses and support networks

Unique Talent

Whilst we just talked about gaps, you may, in fact, have a number of *unique skills, talents* and *attributes* that other candidates simply do not have such as: enjoying computer programming in your spare time, you might have won an award for innovation or helped a relative strip down an engine or build a boat. What other skills and knowledge can you offer to the employer – they may want to hire you for a current role but may also have an eye out for a subsequent promotion. Work with a friend or associate and identify your unique offerings (so-called Unique Selling Point) by completing the table in Figure No. 8.

My unique offerings are:

Area	My unique offering
Knowledge	
Skills	
Attributes/talents	

Figure 8 My unique attributes (unique selling points) (Gatsby 1, 4)

Confidence, Resilience and Attitude

However, skilled and knowledgeable you are, having confidence, resilience and the right attitude will help when looking for a career.

What is Confidence?

Confidence is 'knowing' what you're good at, the value you provide, and acting in a way this conveys that to others. Contrast this with arrogance which typically involves believing you are better in a particular area than you are; or low self-esteem where you believe you are less valuable than you think. The closer your self-assessment is to that reality in the middle, and the more you behave accordingly, then the closer you are to displaying a balance of confidence.

Figure 9 – Ring of Confidence (Gatsby 1, 4)

If you want to raise your confidence to a level that helps (rather than harms) you, it's important to know what you're aiming for. Blindly thinking positive won't necessarily help, and it's possible to go too far (referred to as the Dunning-Kruger effect). In essence, it's when someone overestimates their own abilities, displaying more confidence than their skill level suggests.

Confidence can be seen to have, say, seven dimensions as shown in Figure 10. Let's take these in turn and fill in the blank table items with your reflection on the meaning of the attribute. Sometimes, in life, we lose confidence. But, we can regain this by focusing on our....

Confidence Attribute	What does it mean for you and your job search?
Self-appreciation (Having pride and confidence in yourself; having a feeling that you are behaving with honour and dignity)	
Self-esteem (approval or appreciation of yourself)	
Self-acknowledgement (satisfaction or happiness with yourself)	
Self-ability (understanding who you really are and being a master of yourself – being good at something)	
Self-accountability (being honest with yourself, and answerable and responsible for what you say and do)	
Self-resolve (being self-assured and confident without being aggressive)	

Self-belief	
(the confident way that you feel about your skills, abilities, appearance and behaviour)	

Figure 10 My confidence attributes (Gatsby 1, 4)

If you, currently, have low confidence, why do you specifically believe that is and what steps would you like to take to improve your confidence? Talk to friend and ask them to help you with building your confidence.

Resilience

The word *resilient* comes from the Latin resili, or resilīre, meaning - to spring back, to rebound, to recover. As the world of work and life seem to be faster and faster and expectations become higher and higher, maybe now is the time to step back and take a new approach to developing improved resilience.

Developing Resilience

Personal resilience is the capacity to maintain wellbeing and perform under pressure, to have a ready tool kit to draw on to stay mentally and physically strong and bounce-back from setbacks effectively. Resilience is important for coping well during challenging times.

Stress is the feeling of being out of control, whereas, in contrast, resilience is maintaining control in the face of adversity.

Key benefits of being resilient are:

- Greater flexibility
- Higher energy
- Improved mental agility
- Consistently perform at your highest level
- Have strong relationships and support networks

- Have the capacity to see the future and "go for it"
- Cope with challenges and overcome them
- Have the ability to accept change and see it as an opportunity

These characteristics help you to amplify your performance, your productivity and deliver results along your career path.

Our natural resilience is a combination of personal characteristics and learned skills – and, encouragingly, most people can develop their skills and become more resilient. At times of change and growth, resilience becomes increasingly important for both our individual and business performance.

When searching for work and career opportunities, you might benefit from learning how to develop personal strategies so you can effectively draw on aspects of your personal resilience to cope and respond positively to challenging situations.

You might wish to consider:

- The relationship between pressure, stress, performance, wellbeing and resilience
- Tools to cope better with the pressures you face, developing a more resilient sustainable approach
- A more flexible, adaptable and positive approach to change
- Improved creative problem solving skills
- Strategies to identify and enhance personal strengths whilst working on development needs
- The importance of, and how to set, personal boundaries and manage expectations
- How to become more level-headed and objective under pressure
- How to reduce the risk of illness or burnout by embracing the key principles of physical wellbeing

- How to proactively and positively communicate with others to build, strengthen and maintain positive relationships

You might wish to consider Kumar's CR8 model of resilience which provides a good overview of the key components of resilience and is shown in Figure 11

Figure 11 - Kumar's CR8 model of resilience. (Gatsby 1, 4)

Resilience can be seen to have, say, eight dimensions as shown in Figure 11. Sometimes, in life, we lack resilience. But, we can regain this by focusing on our resilience attributes. Let's take these in turn and fill in the blank table items with your reflection on the meaning of the attribute, figure 12.

Resilience Attribute	What does it mean for you and your job search?
Curiosity	
Communication	
Control	
Change acceptance	
Clarity of focus	
Confidence	
Creativity	
Connectedness	

Figure 12 My resilience attributes (Gatsby 1, 4)

Another way of looking at resilience

Another way to consider resilience is to think about two dimensions, i.e.:

- the level of vulnerability that we demonstrate during an unsettling activity and,
- the time taken to recover from this setback ($T_r - T_0$).

As shown in Figure 13 when some life event, like being out of work, knocks us off track our vulnerability increases and we may also take time to recover from the situation. By either decreasing our level of vulnerability, reducing our recovery time or, a combination of both, enables us to lessen the area of vulnerability, V. It is also possible to recover to a less vulnerable state than before (area v).

During a job search period we may have setbacks, so the more steps we can take to increase our resilience, the better positioned we will be to tackle the next job prospect.

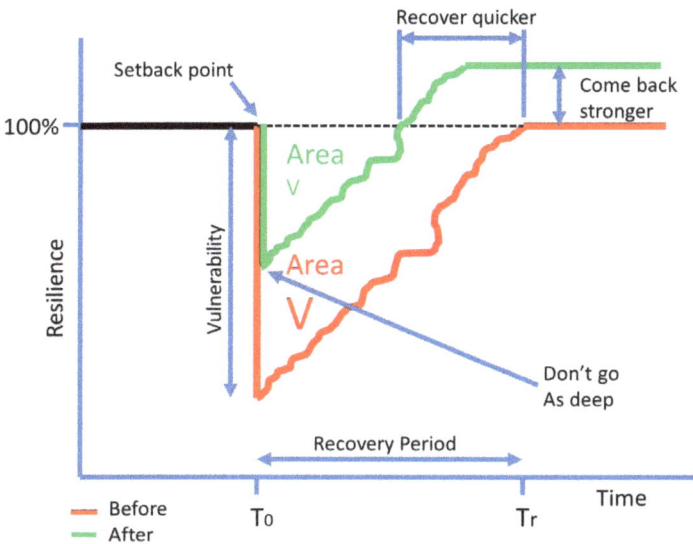

Figure 13 – Resilience area (Gatsby 1, 4)

Attitude

This is such an important aspect of the career management process and I would like to approach it from two angles. Firstly, how our *personal attitude* impacts, positively or negatively, on our ability to secure a suitable role and, secondly, our *attitude to employers and the workplace.*

Personal Attitude

Did you know that there are more negative words than positive words in the English language? Negative experiences, or the fear of them, have a greater impact on most people than positive experiences.

Sometimes when looking for a role we might think that landing that dream job may never happen and we could be in danger of talking ourselves into submission and hopelessness. But what would happen if you could learn to be more optimistic – to focus on the positive rather than the negative, to use positive language, to look for opportunities to find the right role. Take a look at the table in Figure 14 and consider what your negative traits are and, more powerfully, what your positive traits could become.

My negative attitudinal traits are:	
My positive attitudinal traits could be:	

Figure 14 Table –My positive and negative Attitudinal Traits (Gatsby 1, 4)

Attitudes to work, employers and the workplace

If you have not been in work before, or if you have been in work, but not for a long time, it is worth considering what the attitudinal expectations of employers might look like **today**. Take a look at the items in Figure 15 and consider how you see yourself in relation to your attitude to the workplace. These seven elements might serve as prompts to help you think about your workplace behaviour.

Figure 15 Attitudes to the workplace (Gatsby 2)

Now, taking each element in turn, make a few notes in the table, in Figure 16, about where you see yourself at the moment.

Attitudinal item	Context	My current status
Confidence and resilience	How you will stand up to the early pressures of a new workplace	
Desire to succeed	How engaged you will be in the workplace and how hungry you are for success	
Etiquette and Ethics	Manners maketh the man – how will you apply the required standards of behaviour towards others	
Expectation Management and Protocols	Do not expect to be CEO within your first week but have realistic expectations that you can enjoy	
Mentorship/ Guidance	How open will you be to receiving support and guidance in the workplace	
Hygiene, Values	Fundamental rules of hygiene (body odour etc) and core values (showing respect) go a long way towards employee engagement	
People Skills	How you mix with different people and how to communicate clearly with others	

Figure16 – My current status regarding attitudes to the workplace (Gatsby 2)

Decision Making and Goal Setting

How to choose the right career path

Decision making is an important skill for business, life and job hunting. There are processes and techniques to help you improve decision making and the quality of your decisions.

Decision making is more natural to certain people, so they should focus more on improving the quality of their decisions. People that are less natural decision makers are often able to make quality assessments, but then, perhaps, need to be more decisive in acting upon the assessments made.

How to make a no lose decision (after Susan Jeffers)
Sometimes, we hear the phrase, 'be careful, you might make the wrong decision'. This can prevent us from choosing but, by not choosing, we do not do anything! We feel we need to be perfect and might be frightened of making a mistake but, making mistakes could be a good way to learn and improve.

<u>The No-win model</u>
For example, when thinking about which career path to take, as in Figure 17, you stand at the threshold of the decision (choice point) and ask yourself, 'what if it doesn't work?', 'what if this happens?' or 'what if that happens?'

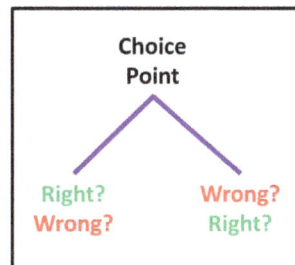

Figure 17 The No-win model of decision making (Gatsby 1, 4)

Choice Point

Right?
Wrong?

Wrong?
Right?

After the decision, the No-win model makes you constantly re-assess the situation hoping you didn't make a mistake and accept the wrong job.

There is, however, another way, the No-lose model. Go back to the choice point and the situation looks like the illustration in Figure 18

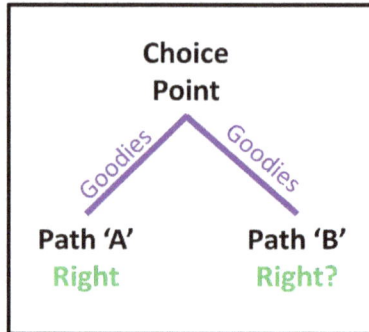

Figure 18 The No-lose model of decision making (Gatsby 1, 4)

There are now two paths, each of which is right. They both have 'goodies', or opportunities to change and improve. Because you are less frightened of making a mistake, you are more confident and therefore more likely to make path A or path B work. The secret is in identifying (and anticipating) the 'goodies'.

Compare the no-win and no-lose models:

No-win: Paralyse yourself with anxiety as you try to predict the future, don't trust your impulses and listen to what everyone else says, feel the heaviness of decision making, create anxiety by trying to control the outcome and, don't correct if the decision is wrong as you have too much invested.

No-lose: Do your research, establish priorities, trust your impulses, lighten up, accept total responsibility, don't protect, just correct where necessary.

Exercise:

Using the no-lose model, consider a key job search decision you are now facing. Write down all the POSITIVE things that can happen by taking either pathway, even if the outcome might not be what you picture.

_____

_____

_____

Pros and cons decision-making template

As mentioned earlier, many people like to have facts to help drive their decisions and sometimes these are hard to pin down. But this can be made easier by using a decision table. By way of example, Figure 19 compares the pros and cons of buying a new car to replace an old car. The pros and cons are purely examples - they are not in any way suggestions of how you should make such a decision. Our decision-making criteria depend on our own personal situations and preferences. Also your criteria (and weighting if appropriate) will change according to the time, situation, and your mind set.

Use whatever scoring method you want to. The example shows scores out of 5, but you can score each item up to 10, or 20 or 100 - whatever makes sense to you personally. Or you can use an 'A/B/C' or three-star scoring method.

Should I replace my old car with a new one?

Pros (for, advantages)	score	Cons (against, disadvantages)	score
Better comfort	4	Cost outlay will mean making sacrifices	5
Lower fuel costs	4	Higher insurance	4
Lower servicing costs	3	Time and hassle to choose and buy it	2
Better for family use	3	Disposal or sale of old car	2
Improved reliability	5	Big decisions like this scare and upset me	3
I'll be a load off my mind	2		
TOTAL Pros	21	TOTAL Cons	16

Figure 19 Pro Con table for car purchase (Gatsby 1, 4)

In this example, on the basis of the number of pros and cons, there seems to be an overall (and quantifiable) advantage in the decision to go ahead and buy a new car.

Notice that with this decision-making method it's even possible to include 'intangible' emotional issues in the pros and cons comparison. For example 'it'll be a load off my mind', and 'decisions scare and upset me'.

A decision-making pros and cons list like this enables a degree of objectivity and measurement, rather than reacting from instinct, or avoiding the issue altogether. Objective measurement may help in making a confident decision and can be really useful in job search activities.

The total scores are the main deciding factor rather than the total number of pros and cons. If the scores are indicating a decision which makes you feel uncomfortable, then check your scoring, and also check that you've not missed out any factors on either side of the table. If the decision makes you feel uncomfortable and this is not reflected in the table, then add it as a factor and give it a score.

Seeking feedback or input from a trusted friend or colleague can be helpful in confirming your factors and their scores.

Exercise: Consider a simple decision, connected to your career search, and complete the Pro Con table in figure 20.

My job search-related decision challenge is:

_____

Pro (for, advantages)	Score	Con (against, disadvantages)	Score
Total		Total	

Figure 20 Blank Pro Con table for career search decision (Gatsby 1, 4)

Using SMART Goals to enhance your job search

Whatever your current situation, setting SMART goals for a job search can help you to find that new position.

Setting goals is more than just having aspirations. Statements like "I will find a new job" or "I will start my own business" are not enough. Setting goals means creating a written plan that includes reasonable, and measurable long-term and short-term objectives. It means setting SMART goals.

There is a **SMART acronym** to explain goal setting. In this case, S.M.A.R.T. refers to goals that are Specific, Measurable, Achievable, Realistic and Time Framed.

Specific: Goals need to be something specific. Most of us have a 'big picture' idea of what we want to achieve. We say, for example, "I will find a new job" or "I want to change career." That's not detailed enough. Saying, "I will re-write my CV this month" is more precise. Now you have something specific to achieve.

Measurable: Goals need to be measurable. For example, when you're out of work it's important to expand your network. But, "making new contacts" is an ambiguous statement. A clearer objective is "I will attend four networking events each month and connect with one person at each event." Or, "I will update my Social Media profile and add one new contact each week." Those are simple, concrete goals that you can measure at the end of each week.

Achievable: Goals need to be reasonable and achievable. At one point or another, many of us have been unemployed. Looking for a job, particularly in an uncertain economy, isn't easy. One of the biggest problems when looking for a job is keeping your morale high. Setting achievable short-term goals that move you towards your medium- and long-term objective of finding a job will help you become more optimistic.

Setting a goal of finding a new job in one month, for example, might not be reasonable. However, applying to at least three companies each week is achievable. It's also important not to set yourself up for failure by setting goals that are too far out of reach.

Realistic: Goals need to be realistic and within reason. Whilst we can have a lot, we probably can't have it all at the same time. It's important to honestly evaluate yourself. Do you have the ability and commitment, at this moment in time, to make your dream come true? What if moving into a new career means going back to College for a short while? Can you work full-time and juggle classes in the evening? Try and be honest with yourself.

Time Framed: Goals need to have a time frame. Having a set amount of time will give your goals some structure. If you're out of work, your savings may dictate your time frame. You may only be able to be unemployed for, say, six months. However, many of us want to change careers or start our own business. Some people spend a lot of time talking about what they want to do, someday. But, without an end date there is no sense of urgency, no reason to take any action today. Having a specific time frame gives you the impetus to get started. It also helps you monitor your progress.

Setting Your S.M.A.R.T. Goals

Setting goals is more than deciding what you want to do. That's only the first step, like picking a destination on a map. To be more successful, you need to map out how you will reach your destination and work out how long it will take you to get there. Now you have the fundamentals of successful goal setting. Keep the SMART acronym in mind to help you remember the basics. The next step is interpreting this process to fit your needs.

Start by determining your end goal or the "big picture" goal. Is it finding a new job or changing career? Once you've decided you're ready to create your plan. Consider your long-term objectives; these are things you want to accomplish by the end of the year. Then establish short-term goals. These include monthly, weekly and even daily targets that will move you towards your long-term objectives.

Be careful not to push yourself too hard or two fast. Whilst you have to stretch your talents to grow, it's important to set reasonable goals. By all means stretch the boundaries but never set yourself up for failure.

The first step to success is in knowing where you want to go. The second step is having a plan to get there. Your long-term goal is your destination. Your short-term goals are your road map. Stick to your plan and you'll be well on your way. Figure 21 depicts a goal option/planning chart to help you focus on where you need to be heading.

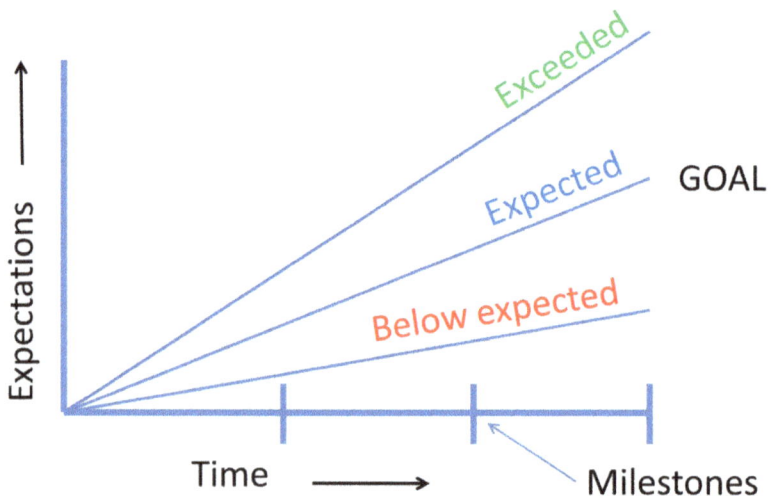

Figure 21 – Goal option/planning chart (Gatsby 1, 4)

Table 22 provides an opportunity for you to think about your current job search SMART goals.

SMART	Job Goal
Specific	
Measurable	
Achievable	
Realistic	
Time Framed	

Figure 22 Table of Your current SMART goals (Gatsby 1, 4)

The Mechanics of Job and Career Searching (RPIF)

It is worth remembering that the overriding object of the job search process is to 'solve the employer's problem', as employers only usually advertise a role to solve a problem (to fill a vacancy).

One way to look at the mechanics of job/career searching is to consider the process in four stages:

Research - Planning - Interview - Follow-up

If we take a look at Figure 23 we can see the four stages in the form of a continuum through which we need to travel, in order.

Research

This implies finding out as much as is reasonably possible about the organisation of interest. We need to determine:

Background – when did the firm start trading, why did they go into this field?

History - what is the company history – is it a family firm or a multi-national?

Sector – which business sectors does the company operate in? Is it electrical, media, textiles, broadcasting etc?

Ethics – does the company have a values statement, do they engage in Corporate Social Responsibility (CSR) and do they appear to work to ethical guidelines?

Number of Employees – how big is the firm? Do they have a small number of employees or many thousands around the globe? This could be an important consideration if you are thinking of a career involving overseas travel.

Direction – what is the current vision and mission for the business?

Financial Status – take a look at Companies House etc and try to find out how the organisation is performing financially.

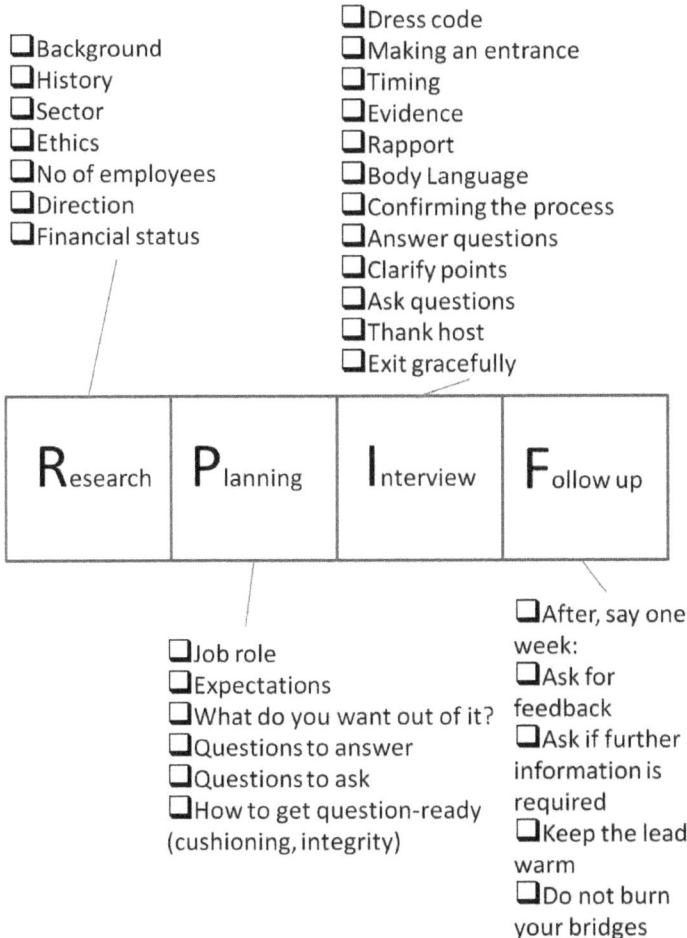

☐Background
☐History
☐Sector
☐Ethics
☐No of employees
☐Direction
☐Financial status

☐Dress code
☐Making an entrance
☐Timing
☐Evidence
☐Rapport
☐Body Language
☐Confirming the process
☐Answer questions
☐Clarify points
☐Ask questions
☐Thank host
☐Exit gracefully

Research	Planning	Interview	Follow up

☐Job role
☐Expectations
☐What do you want out of it?
☐Questions to answer
☐Questions to ask
☐How to get question-ready (cushioning, integrity)

☐After, say one week:
☐Ask for feedback
☐Ask if further information is required
☐Keep the lead warm
☐Do not burn your bridges

Figure 23 Research - Planning - Interview - Follow-up continuum (Gatsby 1, 4)

Planning

This means planning for the interview where the key considerations are:

Job Role – what exactly is the role being advertised? Try and read between the lines to see if the company is looking for an individual with particular skills and experience.

Expectations – what do they expect the new recruit to do?

What we want out of it – if this job is of interest, what exactly are you looking for once in post?

Questions to answer – the interview may be conducted by one person or, more likely, by a panel representing the department of interest, the HR process and a third member. Please see the question list in the chapter on Interview Skills which gives an idea of typical interview questions.

Questions to ask – it is usual during an interview, perhaps towards the end of the process, for the candidate to ask questions of the panel. If you do not have any questions the panel may feel that you lack interest in the organisation or the role. Therefore, prepare three or four questions that would be good to ask. Again, a question list is provided in the chapter on Interview Skills.

How to get question-ready – a few days before the interview, talk with a friend or colleague and prepare answers to potential questions from the panel. In this way, you can answer the questions with authority because you will have practised them and there should be no surprises.

The interview itself

This is your opportunity to convince the interview panel that you are the right person for the job. For this important part of the job search you will need to consider:

Dress Code - It is best not to 'dress down' for an interview, irrespective of the company dress code policy. If you are in any doubt then turn up dressed conservatively. Gentlemen should wear a suit to interviews (this means: a matching jacket and trousers, smart shirt, tie, coordinating socks and smart shoes). Ladies should wear a suit or smart, formal dress.

Making an entrance – this is your chance to build relationships. As the interview starts when you get to within a few hundred metres of the company, you should be thinking about making a strong, confident entrance. This means walking into the company entrance area with purpose and being polite to the team at Reception. Then, when invited into the interview room, be open, friendly and polite.

Timing – ideally you should arrive at the interview location no earlier than 15 minutes before the interview start time. Any earlier and you might just be in the way of the people trying to do their job.

Evidence – when you prepare for the interview, make sure you have good evidence of your accomplishments in a smart folder (bragg file). The evidence could include a few key certificates, a testimonial from a previous employer or a picture of something you have achieved outside of work (perhaps a dry stone wall that you built, a car you renovated or you completing a run for charity). Even if you do not get the opportunity to open the bragg file during the interview, the very fact that you have a smart looking folder with you, shouts professionalism and readiness.

Rapport – early in the interview start to build some rapport with the panel – compliment them on a nice office or interesting paintings around the wall and say something complimentary to the people (without being too obvious). Remember, the interviewers are human beings, they may also be slightly nervous and they would appreciate nice words.

Body Language – just make sure that your body language is open and congruent with your words. Keep an upright stance, try not to slouch and try to maintain appropriate levels of eye contact and interest in the proceedings.

Confirming the process – some interviews are just that – a 40-minute interview; other hiring processes involve additional tests. Whilst the interview process should have been explained to you in the invitation letter, if you are not sure about the process then ask.

Answer questions – Be question-ready and answer the questions truthfully but in a positive way.

Clarify points – if you are not sure about any points made to you, then simply ask for clarification.

Ask questions – be prepared and don't be frightened to ask relevant interesting questions about the company, role and prospects. At my first job interview I asked about the tea-break. Not such a smart move but the interviewer liked my honesty and offered me the job.

Thank the host – at the end of the interview, thank the panel or host for the opportunity and tell them you look forward to hearing from them soon.

Exit gracefully – the interview is not finished until you are out of sight of the building. Therefore, do not slam any office doors, do not be rude in the lift and do not let the CCTV catch you throwing chewing gum in the car park etc. – not that you would!

And finally...

The follow-up

The interview process is not complete until you have a firm understanding of the outcome. This could be: offered the job, offer not forthcoming or, offer given either at a later date or for another role. To ensure that follow-up is done well, consider:

Asking for feedback – wait up to a week and then ask for feedback from the process. If you have not heard anything, just give them a call and, instead of asking how you went on, ask if they need any more information from you at that stage.

Keep the lead warm (if you are still interested in the company/role) – stay in touch as sometimes you might be interviewed for a particular role that you are not offered but, if you made a good impression, you may be offered an alternative role within the business.

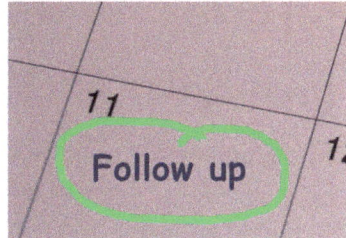

Do not burn your bridges – even if you are rejected for the role, always leave the interview, and the follow-up process, with a positive mindset. As mentioned above, there may be future roles coming up in the company and you want to be firmly on their radar for new opportunities – just be pleasant!

Aligning: CV creation, Cover Letters, Social Media and Job Sites

CVs and Covering letters – advertising your value

Your CV and covering letter is your chance to show an employer the best of what you've got. It's about selling your skills and experience, and showing them you're the right person for the job. How you write your CV and covering letter is up to you, but there are some **basic rules** to follow if you want to create the best impression. Don't be worried if this is your first CV - you'll soon have a professional CV and covering letter that are ready to be sent out to get you interviews.

CV creation – this is really important!!

CV formats – which one? The answer to the question 'which CV format should I use?' is, the format that suits your aims and shows you in the best light. Different CV formats contain mainly the same information but are worded in a different way, in different sections and in a different order. These might seem like small changes to make to your CV, but when employers have hundreds to sift through, every little improvement helps. You can use different CV formats to: draw attention to your *strengths*, *target* a specific job or get across your *career aims* – to change career or get promotion, for example.

Please bear in mind that in all CV formats the personal details, personal profile and qualifications sections remain the same. It's your work history and achievements that change in each format.

A performance CV

This is the most popular type of CV. It highlights job titles and company names, starting with your most recent job and working backwards. However, you would begin with an 'Achievements' section, which highlights impressive achievements that can make you stand out from other candidates. Under each job title you should list your responsibilities in the role.

A functional CV

This is a skills-based CV format. These formats can be useful if you're looking for a career change. This is because they focus on your transferable skills and experience, rather than job titles, companies, and how long ago you gained the experience. In a functional CV you promote your skills and achievements in three to six 'functional headings'. For example, if you're applying for work in a retail role then headings could include 'customer service' and 'sales' – both key skills for any retail role.

Functional CVs are similar to targeted CVs, in that they focus on your skills, but on a functional CV, you choose the title of the three to six skill headings. On a targeted CV the headings are usually 'abilities' and 'achievements'. Therefore, functional CVs can be effective at highlighting your unique combination of skills.

A targeted CV

It's called a targeted CV because you use it to aim for a specific type of job. You only include details that are relevant to the job you're applying for. These are listed in two separate sections: abilities and achievements. A targeted CV is similar to a functional CV, in that it focuses on skills rather than job roles. This can help your major strengths and achievements to stand out.

A student or graduate CV

You might consider using a student or graduate CV if: you're still at school, college or university or you've recently finished a full-time course. With a student or graduate CV you highlight your qualifications first. If you've been in full-time education most of your life your qualifications will probably be your main achievement. If you don't have a lot of work experience, try to make your course work relevant to the skills you would use in the job. For example, you probably use time management, research and IT skills every day. You may also be able to say you're a fast learner, and are up to date with the latest equipment and techniques in your field.

CV content - section by section

Just follow the guidelines below to make sure you've included all the important information an employer may need.

Personal Details - You should include your name, address and contact details. It's up to you whether you include your age, gender, marital status and nationality. Recruiters should be able to make a decision about your skills and abilities without this information.

If you're adding your email address to your contact details make sure that it sounds professional and creates the right impression.

You may also want to add a link to a professional social media website like LinkedIn. If you do, check that the website shows you in a positive light and doesn't contain anything you wouldn't want an employer to see.

Personal Profile - your personal profile is a mini-advert for you and should summarise your skills and qualities, work background, achievements and career aims. It should only be a few lines and must grab the reader's attention. Try to avoid over-used terms, such as 'reliable', 'hard working', 'team player', 'good communication skills' etc. These general terms are heard very often and they don't help an employer to build up a picture of you.

For example, if the job involves working with people, try to highlight relevant, specific people skills such as: negotiating, effectively dealing with demanding customers, presentation skills, handling conflict, or showing empathy. These help the reader build up more of a picture of your skills, knowledge and experience. Be brief - you can go into more detail and highlight examples of your skills in later sections.

When you're summarising your career aims, think about the employer you are sending the CV to. It will hit home with employers if your career aims sound exactly like the kind of opportunities they currently have.

Employment History and Work Experience - if you have been working for a while, you could put your employment history first. If you don't have much work experience, you might like to highlight your education and training. In this section you should start with your present or most recent job and work backwards. You should include employers, the dates you worked for them, job title and your main duties. Provide more detail on the relevant jobs you've had and give examples of the skills you used and what you achieved.

Use bullet-pointed lists and positive language. Try thinking of 'action' words that you can use to describe what you did in your job, like 'achieved', 'designed', 'established', 'supervised', 'co-ordinated', 'created' or 'transformed'. Try to relate your skills and experience to the job description, person specification or what you think the employer is looking for, if you're sending your CV speculatively. Also include any relevant temporary work and volunteering experience.

Avoid unexplained gaps in your employment history. If you had time out travelling, job seeking, volunteering or caring for a relative, include this along with details of what you've learned and skills you've gained.

Education and Training - start with your most recent qualifications and work back to the ones you got at school. Using bullet points or a table include: the university, college or school you went to, the dates the qualifications were awarded and any grades and, any work-related courses, if they're relevant.

Hobbies and Interests – many candidates forget to include relevant detail in this section, which is a shame because **an employer can tell a lot about your personality and qualities from the activities you pursue in your spare time**. You can include hobbies, interests and achievements that are relevant to the job.

For example, if you're involved in any clubs or societies this can show that you enjoy meeting new people. Interests like sports and physical recreation activities can also show employers that you are fit and healthy.

Try to avoid only putting activities that you would do alone like reading, bird-watching or playing video games, unless they relate directly to the job that you are applying for. They may leave employers wondering how sociable you are. Make your activities specific and interesting!

Additional Information - you can include this section, if you need to add anything else that's relevant. Such as explaining that a gap in your employment history was due to travel or family reasons. You could also include other relevant skills here, such as a driving licence or proficiency in foreign languages.

References – I believe it is better to nominate a referee (of course, ask their permission first), rather than state 'referees available upon request'. At least one referee should be work-related or, if you haven't worked for a while, you could use another responsible person who has known you for some time. If you decide to include referee details you should state the relationship of each referee to you – for example 'Sally Jones, Line Manager'.

CV Example

An example CV is shown in Figure 24 and a CV checklist in shown in Figure 25. You can use this as a prompt to help you consider the essential items of your CV.

Mandy Jacobs

16, Spring Street
Halifax
HX2 6ZZ
Tel: 07888999999
E-mail: mandy@chocolate.eu

> Drawing attention to 5 years experience shows a wealth of experience

Profile

An organised, efficient and motivated administrator with five years experience. Communicates confidently and has bags of enthusiasm. Always willing to work hard to complete tasks and support others.

> Highlighted some impressive achievements, within and outside work

Achievements

• Promoted to the role of Chief Administrator to the Managing Director at St. Mary's hospital
• Successfully completed the Duke of Edinburgh Award Scheme
• Completed the Rossendale Triathlon and raised £1,200 for SCOPE charity

> Has Job Titles, Company name and clear responsibilities

Experience

Mid-western Hospital for toxic diseases   Senior Administrator   20015-19
• Provided secretarial support to three consultants specialising in infectious diseases
• Compiled medical reports and articles for weekly reviews
• Arranged the documentation for the Vaccination Seminar in Carlisle
• Typed a number of clinical letters to patients and medical staff

West Bridge District Council   Secretary   2013-2015
• Provided support for local councillors
• Created manifesto articles for election planning teams
• Took minutes of meeting held with Chief Executive and Heads of Service

St. Peters HNS Drop-in Centre   Junior Administrator   2011-2013
• Drafted reports for front line staff and compiled monthly patient numbers summary for Senior Manager
• Updated all records and supported the migration to digital platforms
• Created a new filing system using SQL-one line Star database

> Highlights a logical progression with increasing amounts of responsibility and technical acumen

Figure 24 Example CV (Gatsby 1, 4)

Section	My Key Words
What is my format and why?	
Personal Details content	
Personal Profile content	
Employment history and work experience	
Education and Training	
Interests and Achievements	
Additional Information	
References	
Others...	2 pages A4 on white, concise, easy to read, tailored for the job ...

Figure 25 CV Checklist (Gatsby 1, 4)

Covering Letters - are highly valuable ...

Because the covering letter and CV is the total package – your golden opportunity to sell yourself to employers. Employers are going to be reading your covering letter before your CV so it's important that it makes an impact. Covering letters that create a good first impression are well constructed, don't contain any spelling mistakes or bad grammar, and support what you are saying in your CV.

A good covering letter makes an employer sit up, take notice and want to read your CV. It will have more of an impact if it shows the employer that you have done your research. This means showing you know what the job involves and what they are looking for in an employee. Your letter will need to convince an employer that you want the job and that you're the best person for it.

The Start – grab the reader's attention

You want the employer to read your letter, so remember, this is all about selling yourself. It's essential you make a good impression at the start of your letter.

Address your letter to a specific person - If you're applying on the off-chance that they have a vacancy, first ring the company or organisation to find out the name of the recruiter or the head of the department you want to work for. Don't just address it to Human Resources Department – your application may never get through to the person who's in charge of hiring. If you're replying to an advertisement, address it to the person named in the advert. In both cases, make sure you spell their name correctly and address them with their preferred title, whether it's Mr, Mrs, Ms, Dr, etc.

Explain why you are writing - employers may have to read hundreds of CVs and covering letters so avoid starting yours with 'I am writing'. It's stating the obvious, can become repetitive and may not help your letter to stand out from the crowd. Be clear about what you're applying for, if you're responding to an advertisement. Include the full title of the job, the reference number (if included in the advertisement), and where you saw it advertised. If you're applying 'on spec', be clear about what type of job you're looking for.

Be enthusiastic, show motivation - the start of the covering letter is a good place to show how keen you are to get this job and work for this employer. Many employers will be skim-reading covering letters, so the opening paragraph is your opportunity to impress them with how much you know about their work.

Explain why you believe you are the right person for the company, and what makes you highly motivated to work for this particular employer. Show that you're familiar with their products and services, and recent news about them. You could also explain that you're enthusiastic about working for them because you share their work values, culture and style.

The middle paragraphs (or body) - you have started well, now convince the reader that you know what the job involves, what they want from applicants and that you are the right person. The middle section is where you get into more detail and sell your most relevant skills.

Sell your skills and achievements - do your homework - research the company and the job to find out which are the main skills the employer needs. Think like an employer - which combination of personal qualities, experience, qualifications, and skills would impress? Provide the evidence that you've got them. The covering letter is your opportunity to provide more detail about these key points, more so than in your CV. You might like to include real examples of when you've used these skills. Highlight any major achievements, such as completing training courses, promotions, company awards or any other praise or recognition.

Describe what you can do for them - present your skills in a way that shows how giving you the job will benefit their company. You can do this by cutting down on the number of times you use the word 'I' and increasing the number of times you use 'you' and 'your company'.

Speak and understand their language - use their kind of language. It may seem like a small point, but some organisations prefer formal business language, and others prefer plain-speaking. Have a look at the employer's website, job advertisements and any other communication to try to find out what their preferred language style is. The words and language used in job advertisements can be confusing and often need translation into simple English.

Put yourself in the employer's shoes - it can help if you try to look at your covering letter from the reader's point of view. Imagine you're the employer and ask yourself, 'what do I want from applicants?', 'what would make a candidate stand out?', 'what would be my ideal candidate?', 'why would I hire the person who sent this covering letter?'

*Identify your unique s*elling points (remember, we covered this in the early part of the book) - think about who you'll be competing with and what sets you apart from them. For example, you might have a very specific combination of experience across different work areas. Or, you might have been responsible for winning or completing a big order. Details like this can impress employers and help them build up a picture of who you are. Be positive about who you are and what you have to offer. For example, if you're older you could push your experience, and your ability to learn quickly and hit the ground running. If you're recently out of college or University you could say that your strengths are having new ideas, enthusiasm and a willingness to learn.

Promote your transferable skills - transferable skills are general skills you can use in many different types of job. Selling these skills might be useful to you if you're looking to change career. Think about a job you've done before and the job you want to get into, and try to identify the skills you need for both. Examples of these skills are: working to deadlines, managing budgets and working well with a wide range of people. Transferable skills are general skills you can use in many jobs. You gain these skills from previous jobs, projects, voluntary work, sport, your home life, hobbies, and interests. They enable you to be adaptable and flexible in case you need to change your job.

What are employers looking for? – We alluded to this in the very early chapters of this book. As well as IT, numeracy and good communication skills, some of the other common skills employers want their staff to have are:

Problem solving

Organising

Working to deadlines

Management and leadership

Negotiating

Motivating people

Making decisions

Research skills

In your job applications and interviews, employers will be really impressed if you can provide examples of when you used these skills in different jobs. This shows that you're adaptable and can bring useful skills to a job **straight away**.

How can you show employers you have got the skills they need? - If you are planning a career change, look at the skills mentioned in job adverts. Which have you got and which do you need to work on?

A sample covering letter is shown in Figure 26

Avril Lee
15 Poppy Street
Halifax HX2 7SK
E-mail avril55@hotmail.com
Tel 07777999888

7th January 2020

Mr Harry Smith
Graduate HR director
Scroll Company Ltd
Woodcotes Business Park
Coventry CV22 5HJ

Dear Mr Smith,

Re: Logistics graduate scheme

I would like to apply for the logistics track of your graduate training scheme, advertised on the Prospects.ac.uk website. As requested, I am enclosing my CV.

I am in the final year of my geography degree, expecting a 2:1. Always intending to have a career in business, I have taken modules on the geography of business and GIS modelling. My final-year dissertation is on changing patterns in retail. During my degree, I have developed my analytical skills and ability to read, manage and present data. I have also become familiar with a range of business intelligence sources.

As you can see from my CV I have experience in:
Retail - moving from shelf stacker to checkout operator to team leader in my two years with Tesco. I contributed to the store consistently being in the top five for the region by providing excellent customer service.
Warehouse operations - picking and packing to meet targets over the busy Christmas period.

I have also: Worked in and led teams at Tesco, on course projects and in sports.
Communicated with colleagues at all levels in retail and warehousing.
Solved problems as a team leader, ensuring staff cover and dealing with customer complaints.
Worked flexibly doing both early and late shifts and covering for absence at short notice.
Managed my time when combining study with work and sport.

My semester in Germany exposed me to a different culture and improved my language skills. In addition, my voluntary work with young people has increased my resilience and ability to mix with people from all walks of life.

I look forward to hearing from you.

Yours sincerely

Avril Lee

Figure 26 Sample Covering Letter (Gatsby 1, 4)

A Covering Letter checklist is shown for your use in Figure 27

Section	My Key Words
Sell your Strengths – what are they?	
Make it Personal	
Explain the Gaps	
Explain your Disability	
Speak and understand their language	
Check and Check again	
Keep it brief	
Keep the format consistent	
Grab the reader's attention	
Address your letter to a specific person	
Explain why you're writing	
Be enthusiastic, show motivation	
The middle paragraphs – sell your relevant skills	
Sell your achievements	
Describe what you can do for them	
Others ...	1 page A4 on white, easy to read, tailored for the job, use a computer ....

Figure 27 Covering letter Checklist (Gatsby 1, 4)

Social Media and other job search avenues

Social Media platforms present a really good vehicle for job searching and for making people aware that you are on the lookout for an opportunity. LinkedIn is especially well set up for this activity. If you do not have a LinkedIn account, this is easy to establish. You can then join mutual interest groups and search for decision makers in companies of interest to connect with.

Other career channels are available to you as well, such as Job Boards (Also called employment websites) that deal specifically with employment or careers. Many employment websites are designed to allow employers to post job requirements for a position to be filled. Recruitment Agencies, National Careers Service and C&K Careers also exist to support.

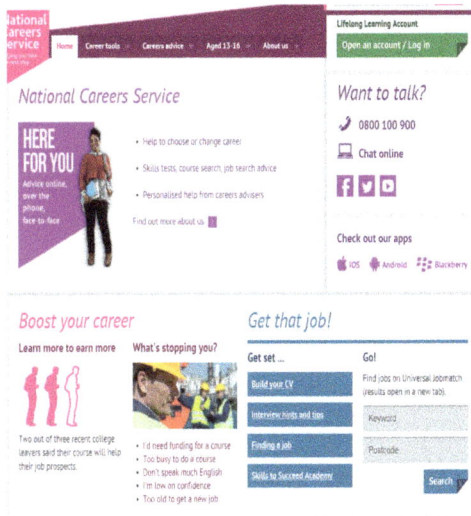

Figure 28 National Careers Service contact details (Gatsby 2)

Interview Skills

So, you have created your CV, produced a compelling covering letter and organised your social media search campaign. Now you have arrived at the interview stage. There are a number of approaches to interviewing and three common types are described here; *conventional, competency-based* and *strengths-based.*

Conventional interviews are essentially a conversation where the interviewers ask a few questions that are relevant to what they are looking for but without any specific process in mind other than getting an overall impression of you as an individual and how you match the job role. Questions can be random and can sometimes be quite open-ended. For example, as seen in the question list in Figure 29, a question such as "What attracted you to this company?" is meant to gather general information about you but does not test any specific skill or competency. In a conventional interview, you may be judged on the general impression that you leave, so the process is therefore likely to be more subjective.

You need to think about the questions that the interview panel are likely to ask you and, similarly, the questions that you are wanting to ask them. In Figures 29 and 30 there are two question lists as just discussed. Now take the time to consider your responses so that you are ahead of the game for your interview.

Typical question	My answer
Why did you apply for this job?	
What attracted you to this company?	
What do you know about our company?	
What do you think our company is aiming to achieve?	
What do you know about our products and services?	
Tell me about yourself?	
What are your hobbies and interests?	
What are your greatest strengths / weaknesses?	
What can you do for us that other candidates can't?	
Why should we hire you?	
Why do you think you are right for this job?	
How would you describe your work style?	
Give evidence of where you worked well in a team	
If you were an animal, what animal would you be and why?	

Figure 29 Interview questions from the panel (Gatsby 1, 4)

Questions from you to the INTERVIEWER

My typical question	Their estimated answer
Which of my skills do you see as most important for the challenges that come with the position?	
Will the company be able to help me develop?	
Can you tell me a little about the team I'll be working with?	
What constitutes success with this position and company?	
Do you see any gaps in my skills or qualifications that I need to fill?	
Do you think I would be right for this job?	
Any others	

Figure 30 Interview questions for the panel (Gatsby 1, 4)

Competency-based interviews

A "Competency" is a concept linking three parameters - *Knowledge, Skills* and *Attitude.* For example - you might have good interpersonal skills (skills), but will not be competent to join a company as Project Manager unless you possess adequate education/experience (knowledge) and the right temperament/behaviour (attitude). Competency-based interviews use questions designed to test one or more specific areas. The answer is then matched against pre-determined criteria and marked accordingly. For example, the interviewers may want to test your ability to deal with stress by asking first how you generally handle stress and then asking you to provide an example of a situation where you worked under pressure.

Which skills and competencies do competency-based interviews test?

Many interviews now are competency-based which means that the interviewer will be looking for you to answer questions about your abilities and experience **in the context of actual events**. It is worth preparing in advance at least two examples for each competency as the recruiter might ask for a second example, particularly if you have already quoted one on an application form.

The list of skills and competencies that can be tested varies depending on the post that you are applying for. For example, for a Personal Assistant post, skills and competencies would include communication skills; ability to organise and prioritise; and ability to work under pressure. For a senior manager position, skills and competencies may include an ability to influence and negotiate; an ability to cope with stress and pressure; ability to lead; and the capacity to take calculated risks.

Here is a list of the more common skills and competencies that you may be asked to demonstrate:

Skills and competencies for competency-based interviews		
Adaptability	Delegation	Leveraging diversity
Compliance	External Awareness	Organisational awareness
Communication	Flexibility Independence	Resilience and tenacity Risk-taking
Conflict management	Influencing Integrity Leadership	Sensitivity to others Team work
Creativity and innovation		
Decisiveness		

Figure 31 Skills and competencies for competency-based interviews (Gatsby 1, 2, 4)

What kind of competency-based interview questions could you be asked? Although most questions tend to ask for examples of situations where you have demonstrated specific skills, they can appear in different formats. Examples include:

- How do you ensure that you maintain good working relationships with your senior colleagues?

- Give us an example of a situation where you had to deal with a conflict with an internal or external client.

- Tell us about a situation where you made a decision and then changed your mind.

In many cases, the interviewers will start with a general question, which they will follow-up with more specific, example-based questions.

For example:

- How do you manage upwards?

- Give us an example of a situation where you had a fundamental disagreement with one of your superiors.

The key in answering all questions is that you are required to "demonstrate" that you have the right skills by using examples based on your prior experience, and not just talk about the topic in a theoretical and impersonal manner.

How competency-based interview questions are marked

Before the interview, the interviewers will have determined which type of answers would score positive points and which types of answers would count against you. For example, for questions such as "Describe a time when you had to deal with pressure", the positive and negative indicators may be as follows:

Positive indicators	Negative indicators
Demonstrates a positive approach towards the problem	Perceives challenges as problems
Considers the wider need of the situation	Attempts unsuccessfully to deal with the situation alone
Recognises their own limitations	Used inappropriate strategies to deal with pressure/stress
Is able to compromise	
Is willing to seek help when necessary	
Uses effective strategies to deal with pressure/stress	

Figure 32 Positive and Negative indicators (Gatsby 1, 4)

In some cases, negative indicators are divided into two further sections: *minor negative indicators*, i.e. those which are negative but which don't matter so much; and *decisive negative indicators* i.e. those for which they won't forgive you e.g. not asking for help when needed.

Marks are then allocated depending on the extent to which your answer matches those negative and positive indicators. An example of a marking schedule is shown in Figure 33.

Mk	Grade	Reason
0	No evidence	No evidence reported
1	Poor	Little evidence of positive indicators Mostly negative indicators, many decisive
2	Areas for concern	Limited number of positive indicators Many negative indicators, one or more decisive
3	Satisfactory	Satisfactory display of positive indicators Some negative indicators but none decisive
4	Good to excellent	Strong display of positive indicators

Figure 33 Marking schedule example for Positive and Negative indicators (Gatsby 1, 4)

If the interviewers feel there are areas you have failed to address, they may help you along by probing appropriately. For example, in answering the question *"Describe an example of a time when you had to deal with pressure"*, if you focused on how you dealt with the practical angle of the problem but you forgot to discuss how you managed your stress during and after the event, the interviewers may prompt you with a further question such as *"How did you handle the stress at the time?"* This would give you an opportunity to present a full picture of your behaviour.

Preparing for a competency-based interview

Preparation is crucial if you want to be able to answer competency-based questions without having to think too much on the spot on the day of the interview. A few preparation pointers are shown below:

1. Make sure you understand which skills and competencies will be tested. It sounds obvious, but some job/person specifications can be a little vague and you will need to do some thinking in order to ensure that the examples you give will hit the mark. For example, the person specification may say that you need to have "good communication skills in dealing with third parties". For someone who works in customer service and is expected to handle complaints, this will most likely involve a mix of empathy/understanding as well as an ability to be assertive in a nice way when required; however for someone applying for a commercial law post, this will most likely involve an ability to explain complex matters in a simple way.

2. Identify examples from your past experience which you can use to demonstrate that you possess the skills and competencies that you are being asked to demonstrate. You do not have to find over-complicated examples; in particular the outcome of the story does not have to be extraordinary; what matters most is that the role you played in reaching the outcome was substantial.

The STAR Method

You could learn to narrate your story using the STAR method. This means setting the scene, explaining how you handled the situation by placing the emphasis on your role, and detailing the outcome.

This method ensures that your answers are succinct and that you do not to go off on a tangent.

S	Situation	Briefly set the scene
T	Task	Describe what was required
A	Activity	What did you do and why?
R	Result	What was the outcome?

Figure 34 The STAR Method (Gatsby 1, 4)

As shown in Figure 34, STAR is an effective response technique for competency-based questions, and is a proven method for structuring your answers so that they are relevant and focused. Make sure that you listen to the question, take a moment to consider your answer and reply in the following way:

Situation: Briefly set the scene to give the interviewer some context. Ensure that you refer to a specific instance and real people. Do not generalise about typical situations and avoid being vague.

Task: Explain what your responsibility was in this situation and what the challenges and constraints were.

Activity: Describe what you did and why and always focus on *your* contribution to the task, not what your colleague or your team did.

Result: Always try to end your answers on a positive outcome. If the situation did not end particularly well, explain what you have learnt from the experience to turn it into a positive example.

Competency-Based Interview Questions

Competency-based interview questions vary widely between sectors and depending on the level of responsibility to which you are applying. The type of competencies against which you will be assessed also depends on the actual post and the company who is interviewing you. For example, some companies view leadership as a competency on its own whilst others prefer to split leadership between a wide range of components (creativity, flexibility, strategic thinking, vision, etc). You will find below a spectrum of competency-based interview questions, ordered by competency. The list is by no means complete but will give you an idea of what you can expect to be asked.

Adaptability - Adjusts to changing environments whilst maintaining effectiveness.
Q: Tell us about the biggest change that you have had to deal with. How did you cope with it?

Compliance - Conforms to company policies and procedures
Q: Tell us about a time when you went against company policy. Why did you do it and how did you handle it?

Communication - Communicates effectively, listens sensitively, adapts communication to audience and fosters effective communication with others.

Verbal
Q: Describe a time when you had to win someone over who was reluctant or unresponsive.

Listening
Q; Tell us about a time when you were asked to summarise complex points.

Written
Q: How do you feel writing a report and how does it differ from preparing an oral presentation?
Conflict management - Encourages creative tension and

differences of opinions. Anticipates and takes steps to prevent counter-productive confrontations. Manages and resolves conflicts and disagreements in a constructive manner.

Q: Tell us about a time when you felt that conflict or differences were a positive driving force in your organisation. How did you handle the conflict to optimise its benefit?

Creativity and Innovation -Develops new insights into situations; questions conventional approaches; encourages new ideas and innovations; designs and implements new or cutting edge programs/processes.

Q: Tell us about a situation where you trusted your team to derive a new approach to an old problem. How did you manage the process?

Decisiveness - Makes well-informed, effective, and timely decisions, even when data are limited or solutions produce unpleasant consequences; perceives the impact and implications of decisions.

Q: When is the last time that you have refused to make a decision?

Q: Tell us about a time when you had to make a decision without knowledge of the full facts.

Delegation - Able to make full and best use of team members, providing appropriate support.

Q: What type of responsibilities do you delegate? Give examples of projects where you made the best use of delegation.

Resilience and Tenacity - Deals effectively with pressure; remains optimistic and persistent, even under adversity. Recovers quickly from setbacks. Stays with a problem/line of thinking until a solution is reached or is no longer reasonably attainable.

Q: Tell us about a situation where things deteriorated quickly. How did you react to recover from that situation?

Risk-taking - Takes calculated risks, weighing up pros and cons appropriately.
Q: What is the biggest risk that you have taken? How did you handle the process?

Sensitivity to others/empathy - Aware of other people and environment and own impact on these. Takes into account other peoples' feelings and needs.
Q: Tell us about an unpopular decision that you made recently? What thought-process did you follow before making it? How did your colleagues/clients react and how did you deal with their reaction?

Teamwork - Contributes fully to the team effort and plays an integral part in the smooth running of teams without necessarily taking the lead.
Q: Tell us about a situation where you played an important role in a project as a member of the team (not as a leader).

By considering the above examples and applying the STAR method of answering you will be in a strong position to handle competency-based interviews.

A typical competency-based question and STAR-based answer might take the following form:

Question
Tell us about a time when you led a team to bring a project to a satisfactory conclusion.

STAR answer
Situation – a group of six of us were in a forest conducting a hike for our Duke of Edinburgh Award. One of our team members fell over and badly sprained their ankle and could not continue on foot.

Task – as we were, at least, 2 miles from the nearest road, our task was to get our friend safely to a hospital so she could receive medical attention.

Activity – I had the presence of mind to talk with the remaining members of the group and gave each one a task (two friends were asked to find two stout branches that would serve as stretcher poles. Another friend was asked to sit with our injured colleague and re-assure her. We all took of our jackets and threaded the two branches through our jackets to make a stretcher on which we carefully placed our injured friend). We checked our map for the nearest main road and set a compass bearing towards it.

Result – after 40-minutes of careful walking we reached a main road, flagged down a passing motorist and transferred our patient into the car. Two of us accompanied the driver and our friend received first class medical attention in a local medical centre.

Strengths-based interviews

A number of large organisations already use strengths-based interviewing as part of their graduate recruitment process.

What is a strength-based interview?

A strengths-based interview focuses on what you enjoy doing, rather than what you can do as in a competency-based interview. But don't be fooled, while you're talking about what you like and dislike the employer is learning about what you're good at, and not so good at. Strengths-based interviewing has its foundations in positive psychology. The theory is that by identifying your strengths and matching them to the role you'll be happier in your work, perform better, learn quicker and stay with the company for longer.

Unlike their competency-based counterparts, strengths-based interviews are more personal and allow recruiters to gain a genuine insight into the personalities of candidates and to see if they'd be a good 'fit' for the company. They also allow you, as the interviewee, to be selected on the basis of your natural abilities.

Why use strengths-based interviews?

The strengths-based approach is particularly useful when recruiting individuals who don't have much work experience and companies such as Aviva, BAE Systems, Barclays, Cisco, EY, Nestle, Royal Mail and Unilever use strengths-based interviews as part of their graduate recruitment process.

Another reason that employers are beginning to favour a strengths-based approach is that candidates have less opportunity to prepare and rehearse their answers, meaning that interview questions are more likely to bring out the genuine interest, motivation and aptitude of interviewees. An added benefit is that most people come across best when they're talking about things they enjoy so strengths-based

interviewing makes for a more pleasurable interview experience all round, for both the interviewer and interviewee.

Strengths-based interview questions

The strengths that employers look for depend on the job. For example, for a customer-facing role you'd be expected to enjoy, and be confident in, communicating with a variety of people and have experiences to back this up. Supporting examples could include volunteering with community groups, being a member of your university debating or social team or having some part-time retail work. As the recruiter is trying to get a sense of who you are in a short space of time, expect to answer a lot of questions. You could be asked as many as 20-30 questions in an hour-long interview.

Here are some examples of strengths-based interview questions:

What do you like to do in your spare time?

What energises you?

How would your close friends describe you?

Do you prefer the big picture or the small details?

What are you good at?

Have you ever done something differently the second time around?

Do you think this role will play to your strengths?

How to answer strengths-based interview questions

Strength questions don't have a right or wrong answer, so don't worry on that account. It is however important that you answer all questions honestly, failing to do so will give the interviewer a false impression of you. Just like in any other interview you'll need to include examples to back up and illustrate your responses. You can draw these examples from all areas of your life including your studies, work experience, previous employment, volunteering or extra-curricular activities.

If you're asked to identify your weaknesses stay away from generic responses such as 'I'm a perfectionist'. Think of things that you've struggled with in the past and select a real weakness, such as a lack of organisational skills which impacts on your ability to meet deadlines, or low confidence when it comes to networking or public speaking. Ensure that you explain how your strengths compensate for this weakness and WHAT YOU'RE DOING TO OVERCOME ANY SHORT FALLS. For example, for a lack in organisational skills you could explain how you're using alerts and apps on your Smartphone to positive effect and how a combination of lists, spreadsheets and a day planner help keep you on track. Always end your responses on an upbeat note.

When you're answering their questions, interviewers will be taking note of your body language and tone of voice, which can provide clues to your sincerity. If you're genuinely describing something you enjoy you'll be animated and your enthusiasm and motivation will shine through.

Preparing for a strengths-based interview

Many recruiters believe it's impossible to prepare for a strength-based interview. The technique is designed to prevent candidates from planning or rehearsing their responses, plus, you have no idea what you're going to be asked. However, just because you can't practise your answers doesn't mean that there aren't other things you can do to make yourself interview ready.

No matter which interview method is used, you still need to do your research into the company and the role. Read the person specification to identify what strengths and qualities the company is looking for. Then make a list of your own strengths. Include your academic, work and social achievements, when you're usually at your best and what motivates you. Think about activities you enjoy doing, subjects you've enjoyed learning about and also about things you like less. Consider how all these strengths could be used to the advantage of the organisation you are wishing to work for.

Telephone and Video Interviews

As well as the physical, human-interaction, interviews mentioned above, you may also be invited to take part in a telephone interview or a video interview.

Telephone Interviews

A phone interview is often a screening exercise with the employer checking some basic information such as your reasons for applying and your availability to attend for interview. Here are five Telephone Interview Tips.

1. Take it as seriously as a face-to-face Interview

As this is an interview, you need to treat it like one. Of course, that means being ready! When your interview is first scheduled, make sure you set aside time BEFORE the interview to prepare for it. If it's an early morning interview, make sure you're "in the mood" before the phone rings. Get up early, get moving, get your vocal cords warmed up and make a cup of tea or coffee, or have a glass of water to hand.

This is just as much a mental game as a physical game and dressing the part (even if they can't see you) can really help you get into the right frame of mind to get the job. Dress the part and stand up to facilitate improved breathing.

2. Focus and eliminate distractions

Make sure you're not distracted. Turn off the television and other potential distractions (dishwasher, cooling fans etc). The interviewer can tell if you're distracted and, consequently, delaying your answers because you're focusing on other activities.

Find a comfortable space and have all your prepared material in easy reach. If you're conducting the interview at home and you're not alone, make sure everyone knows you're going to be busy for a while and ask them to give you some privacy and quiet. Present yourself in the most professional way possible, from the first "Hello," to the last "Goodbye."

3. Listen and don't dominate the conversation

Yes, this is an interview which means they're going to be asking you questions, but it's also an opportunity to show your potential employer that you're good at listening too. Talk, but don't dominate the conversation. Let the interviewer guide the conversation. Answer the questions, but don't turn it into a one sided monologue. This is as much about you getting to know them as it is about them getting to know you.

Ask a few follow-up questions but don't try to be the interviewer. It helps to reinforce to the interviewer that you're truly interested in the company and the job and that you've paid attention during the interview. Make sure you breathe through your diaphragm and speak clearly. More importantly, smile - as a smile can be heard over the phone. You will also feel better when you smile.

4. Slow down

Pause and take a breath between the interviewer asking you a question and you starting to answering it. Sometimes people ask questions but then continue to talk rather than waiting for you to answer. Give the interviewer a couple of seconds after each question before you start so you don't both end up talking at once which might be awkward. Sometimes it is difficult to gauge when to answer as the line goes quiet but you do not know what is happening at the other end - are you waiting for them, are they waiting for you? Also, as you pause it gives you a chance to think about what you're going to say next.

5. Send a Thank You e-mail after the telephone interview

This telephone stage is about making a good first impression and the fact that you're doing this all via phone makes the follow-up even more critical. Finish your phone call on a positive note, but follow up in a timely manner with a thoughtful thank you email after your interview. Let the interviewer know you appreciated their time on the phone, that you enjoyed the experience and that you are interested in the next phase. It will help you stand out and reinforce to them that you're truly interested in the position. Above all be mindful that the focus here is on how you add value to the company, not just what your past experiences are and what you're good at.

Video Interviews

Video Interviews help employers to filter candidates at an early stage and may also be used to assess candidates if the role involves customer interfacing via visual media. Video interviews are an increasingly popular way of assessing candidates across all job sectors. Video interviews can vary in style and length. You may be

asked to answer pre-recorded questions with an allotted time given for each response. Or the interview may be live, in a similar format to a traditional interview and carried out on a platform such as Skype or FaceTime.

The obvious benefits of a video interview are the money and time savings for both the interviewer and the candidate. It also means that the interviewer and their colleagues can watch the interview again later. There may also be potential disadvantages with video interviews such as unreliable connectivity and time delays. In addition, not everyone will be comfortable in front of a camera and this may put some candidates off the process. However, with a little bit of preparation these issues can be overcome.

Here are five tips for a strong Video Interview.

1. Be prepared

Talking on camera doesn't come naturally to some people so it's important to do some test runs to help you become familiar. Record yourself and replay the video to see how you look and sound. This is a great opportunity to review your body language and make sure the environment looks good.

Research information needs to be kept away from the camera and try not to fiddle with your notes during the interview as the rustling of paper will affect the sound quality and may distract the interviewer.

2. Choose your location

Plan well in advance where you're going to conduct the interview. Use a quiet location, where you won't be disturbed . Make sure the room you choose is tidy and use a clean and simple background so that the interviewer focuses on you.

3. Dress professionally

You may be at home but this is still a job interview and your opportunity to make a compelling first impression. This means dressing appropriately and you should wear the same outfit you would have worn for a face-to-face interview, as outlined in the chapter on the mechanics of job searching.

4. Use positive body language

Avoid slouching, moving too much or overusing mannerisms like touching your face or stroking your hair. The interviewer will be looking for you to make good eye contact, smile, listen and take an interest in what is being said. To help you do this, your camera should be at eye level and you should look into it rather than at the screen.

5. Optimise the technology

Have a think about the lighting in the room you will use and ensure you don't produce shadows. Use natural light from a nearby window or place a lamp in such a position that gives clear light.

A few days before the interview you should test the computer, camera and any software that you've been asked to use. Make sure the picture is clear and the sound quality is good. It's also worth checking your internet connection.

No matter the interview technique you still need to do your research into the company and the role. Read the person specification to identify what strengths and qualities the company is looking for. Then make a list of your own strengths. Include your academic, work and social achievements, when you're usually at your best and what motivates you. Think about activities you enjoy doing, subjects you've enjoyed learning about and also about things you don't like doing and your weaknesses. Think about how all these strengths could be used to the advantage of the organisation you're hoping to work for.

Other tests requirements

Some organisations may also ask you to complete a few tests, either in the company or at an Assessment Centre. These tests are usually designed to assess your ability to reason things out and a range of tests include: Logical, Verbal, Non-verbal, Numerical, Aptitude, Spatial awareness etc.

Logical reasoning

There are numerous types of logical reasoning test and many of these are used interchangeably. These tests tend to be similar in their layout and methodology, but with subtle and important differences. Common logical reasoning tests include:

Inductive reasoning: Inductive reasoning is the ability to reach general conclusions based on perceived patterns observed in specific events. Inductive logic is often used in everyday life and is therefore practical to a work place environment. In these tests you may be provided with a series of diagrams with an evident pattern. You will need to identify the pattern in the sequence of diagrams and select the next diagram in the sequence.

Deductive reasoning: Deductive reasoning involves a general rule or principle that leads to a specific conclusion. These tests will evaluate and measure your ability to make logical arguments and draw sound conclusions based on provided data, as well as identify flaws in a piece of information. As a result this is a useful tool in selection procedures as this type of reasoning will be used in the workplace.

Abstract reasoning: Abstract reasoning, also known as conceptual reasoning measures your lateral thinking ability. In these tests you will be tested on your ability to identify relationships, patterns and trends. You may be provided with a series of images that follow a logical sequence or underlying rules. This may include following a rule in a sequence, identifying a code or finding a missing diagram.

Diagrammatic reasoning: Diagrammatic reasoning is a specific form of abstract reasoning. Tests which assess this ability will typically show a flowchart of diagrams and symbols, with an input and an output. You may be asked to identify which inputs effect outputs, and therefore generate a specific output based on those rules.

Critical thinking: Critical thinking tests are a type of verbal critical reasoning task which assesses various different types of logical reasoning in arguments, assumptions and conclusions. Typical logical abilities tested include analysing arguments, making inferences and evaluating conclusions.

Example: Which of the nine squares on the right would best fit in the space in the main square?

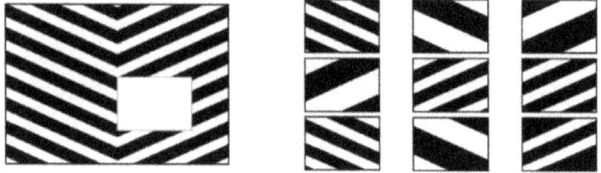

Verbal reasoning

Employers often use verbal reasoning tests because they are better at predicting candidates' job performance than interviews, CVs and other traditional methods of selection.

Employers use your verbal reasoning score, together with other selection factors such as interview performance, to help them decide who is most suitable for the role. Verbal reasoning tests used in selection usually take the form of a written passage followed by a series of questions with possible **True, False** or **Cannot Say** responses. It is important that, if you have these tests, you know and appreciate the meaning of each response if you are to score highly.

True - The statement follows logically given the information contained within the passage.

False - The statement cannot logically follow given the information contained within the passage.

Cannot Say - It is not possible to determine given the information contained within the passage alone; i.e. more information would be required to say for certain.

Example Verbal Reasoning test question

Please read the passage below and answer the questions that follow.

In the 16th century, an age of great marine and terrestrial exploration, Ferdinand Magellan led the first expedition to sail around the world. As a young Portuguese noble, he served the king of Portugal, but he became involved in the quagmire of political intrigue at court and lost the king's favour. After he was dismissed from service by the king of Portugal, he offered to serve the future Emperor Charles V of Spain.

The 16th century was an age of great [   ] exploration

Numerical reasoning

With thousands of job applicants to choose from, it's common for employers to use aptitude testing to sift the good candidates from the mediocre. The most common way for employers to use numerical reasoning tests is **online**, after they have accepted CVs or initial application forms. If a candidate passes online tests, larger employers tend to then invite them to an **assessment centre**. Often employers ask candidates to sit a repeat test at the assessment centre to verify that they are indeed the same person who scored that great score on the online test.

What is the missing number that should replace the question mark?

Figure 35 Example Numerical Reasoning question (Gatsby 1, 4)

?	7	10
6	9	...
8	...	14

As well as taking example tests, candidates can read the advice on how these tests work and what they measure. By taking example numerical reasoning tests candidates will become familiar with the question format. Luckily most employers use a similar format of numerical reasoning test, which means it's easy to get some realistic practice beforehand.

The great thing about the numerical reasoning tests used for employment selection is that they are not the same as a maths test. There is no need to remember formulae or write long proofs.

The important characteristics of a numerical reasoning test are:

Multiple choice answers - no longhand answers or showing your working-out.

No prior knowledge required - no equations to memorise (or surreptitiously write on your arm).

Strict time limits - some are generous while some are very short.

Relevant to the workplace - modern tests are based on the kind of numerical information you would deal with in the job.

Based on only the information given - you should not make assumptions about data you are **not** given and Universities often give help with preparation for assessment centres.

Sample assessment tests can be obtained from: shldirect.com, wikijob.co.uk or practiceaptitudetests.com etc.

Communications skills and People skills are the keys to success

In the search for a job, communicating with and relating to people is important.

Communications Skills

Communicating with others - It is not just about the words, it is also about voice tonality and body language. Way back in 1964, a professor at U.C.L.A by the name of Albert Mehrabian said that any message has three key components; words, voice tonality and body language and that words account for only 7% of the message, voice tonality makes up 38% which means that a whopping 55% is due to how we present with our gestures and body language. Considering these three components, I like to make the analogy that 'people will, perhaps, forget what you said, they may forget what you did but they will never forget how you made them feel.

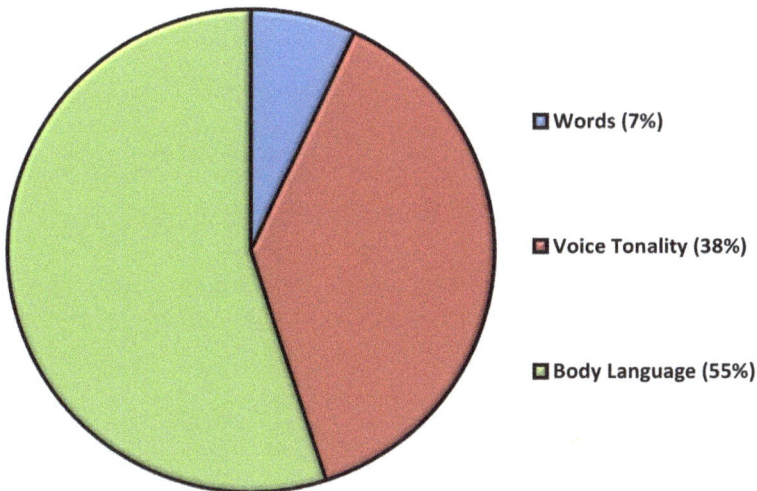

■ Words (7%)

■ Voice Tonality (38%)

■ Body Language (55%)

Figure 36 Mehrabian Message Circle (Gatsby 1, 4)

<u>Powerful questioning</u> - when we ask questions of other people it is good to ask them in a structured order, using the 5 why's techniques (up to 5 consecutive 'why' questions to further understand the other person's point of view). You can use their responses as links and bridges to the subsequent question.

<u>Active listening</u> – communication is a two-way exchange and *listening actively* is as important as delivering the message.
It also ensures that the message has been received and understood. People will know that we are actively listening to them if we nod, say yes, 'a-ha' or paraphrase the message back to them. If we go beyond *active listening* then we can listen *generatively*. This means we remember the information being given to us for future use in relationship building.

<u>Imparting knowledge successfully</u> - making information clear means being confident with our ideas, being succinct, communicating the data and seeking clarification of understanding. As we get towards the end of a conversation it is useful to check that both parties have understood the message and are clear on any action that needs to be taken.

Presenting to others

During your interview/assessment process you may be asked to give a short presentation to a group. Presenting information to people can be quite daunting and many studies have shown that this is one of the most stressful situations in which people may find themselves. However, with a few tools and techniques it is possible to become highly competent at, and comfortable with, presenting.

How to overcome our presentations challenges

There are a number of techniques that we can use to overcome our challenges, such as:

Learning to relax

Improving our breathing (ideally through our diaphragm)

Practising new ways of thinking

Building confidence in our own ability (one of the presuppositions of Neuro Linguistic Programming (NLP), for example, is that: anything which has been achieved is a process and, therefore, it can be learnt)

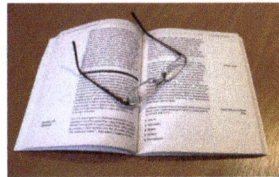

Practice until it becomes automatic (new behaviours take time to learn)

Others ......

More presentations hints and tips include:

Be yourself (but be your best-self).

Have confidence, you are as good as the next person (and, actually, your audience usually want you to succeed).

Stay grounded, do not walk around too much. When you do walk, do it with purpose.

Try to keep the focus on yourself and not on any visuals.

Maintain good eye contact with members of the group (try to determine their eye colour).

Know your material really well.

Have a positive feeling about the subject.

Show sincerity.

Project the value of your message to your audience.

A smile on your face can be heard in your voice.

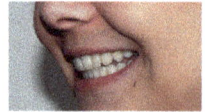

The 'K' factor – speaking words beginning with K force you to smile.

<u>I can't remember what to say – yes you can!</u>

Some people feel that they cannot remember what to say during a presentation. This is understandable, but try to memorise segments of your talk using a string of pictures in your head.

Techniques include:

Memory Stacking
Memory Journey (Palace), or
Memory Pegging.

Presentation structure

It is good for your presentation to have some structure and, as a minimum, it should contain the following:

Opening – attract immediate interest from the group.

Message – state your message clearly.

Evidence – establish credibility and gain respect by using evidence.

Closing – leave the audience with a positive, memorable

impression.

First and lasts are remembered (primacy & recency).
It is worth focusing on these at construction, preparation and delivery of a presentation.

The 'ta-dah' moment
Conclude, if you can, with a 'ta-dah' moment so that your audience will be talking about this as they leave, and for some time thereafter.

Try to ensure that your ta-dah moment comes after any Q and A session.

Handling Questions

Presenting information (like most forms of communication) is a two-way process. Therefore, during or sometimes after a presentation, your audience will want to ask questions about your topic. Here are a few things to consider when handling questions:

Get question-ready
In the days leading up to your presentation, review your topic and anticipate any questions that might come up. Try asking a trusted friend of fellow student to think of questions that people might ask. Take this bank of questions and formulate succinct answers to them and then practise the answers.

Be in control
Towards the end of your presentation (but not at the end), confidently ask for questions by saying 'who has the first question?'. This shows that you welcome their input and that you

are not frightened of having a dialogue.

<u>When the questions come up:</u>
Acknowledge them by thanking the questioner. If the question was asked in a low voice you can repeat the question so that the rest of the room can benefit (this also buys you a couple of seconds of thinking time).

If the question is not totally clear then just ask the questioner to repeat the question (again, this buys you some thinking time).

Think about the question for a few seconds, then:

Cushion the question if necessary. If a question is topical you can say a few words about the relevance.

If the question is aggressive or challenging in a negative sense then cushion with "I hear what you say, I respect your opinion, that's an interesting point of view", but never say 'you are wrong'.

When you have cushioned the question you can respond in a positive, factual way but never start this response with 'but' or 'however'. Just start with 'in my opinion...' or ' research shows that ....'

Answer truthfully. If you don't know the answer just say so. This will buy you more credibility than trying to make up an answer.

After the Q and A session you can conclude with your big finish. It can be risky to end on a Q&A in case you get a question from that insecure smart Alec.

Presenting and Pitching

How to sell yourself to an employer - If you are asked to make a pitch to an employer, or if you meet a potential employer in an elevator, you could use the **AIDA** formula:

Your Elevator Pitch

When delivering your elevator pitch the following format might be useful. Remember Verdi's Nubian Princess, **AIDA**.

A – Attention: attract the attention o f the audience (be dramatic).

I – Interest: raise interest by focusing on and demonstrating advantages (features).

D – Desire: convince the audience that they want and desire what you can offer them and that it will satisfy their needs and solve their problems.

A – Action – lead the audience towards action and leave a memory hook.

Attention

Interest

Desire

Action

Figure 37 AIDA pitch preparation table (Gatsby 1, 4)

Your Pitch can be developed by using the table in Figure 37

Having recorded the key theme of your AIDI pitch, you can develop your story using the pitch preparation narrative, Figure 38

Topic: _____

My opening statement is:

_____

_____

My key message is: _____

_____

My supporting evidence is:

_____

_____

My closing line is:

_____ _____

_____

Figure 38 Pitch preparation narrative (Gatsby 1, 4)

It's not WHAT you know - the value of networking

It's not just WHAT you know, it's also WHO you know and networking can be a useful method of meeting the right people.

If networking is a bit of a mystery to you or if you hate walking into a room full of strangers and actually talking to people and trying to think of something to say, then you are not alone. But, if you are looking to put bread on the table and have a stimulating career then your best chance of success might just be through meeting other people and that means NETWORKING.

Here are some useful tips to consider.

Sometimes we resist putting ourselves forward or we don't look for networking opportunities. Then, when such opportunities are created, or just happen, we often don't make the best impression or we say the wrong things. However, with some simple tips and a bit of practice, you could be an effective networker, enabling you to build a circle of contacts that can help to positively influence your career journey.

In this chapter there are some **Hot Tips** to help you dispel your fears, build your confidence and support you in becoming an effective networker. We cover: preparing for a meeting, asking the right questions, recognising a business opportunity, building relationships with the people you meet, eliminating your doubts and concerns and how to make confident follow up phone calls.

When and where to Network

You can network almost everywhere you go; talk to people in supermarkets, trains, buses, in the evenings, at weekends. Remember you do not know who the people are or who they know so be prepared at all times. Opportunities are all around you and some of the best contacts come from the most unexpected places. Attend the most appropriate network events where your target customers/ contacts are likely to be. Otherwise you may be wasting your time, energy and money.

Before a networking event

Before attending any networking session you need a clear set of objectives. Before the event, try and find out as much as you can about who will be there and how you can help some of the people who will be present. Check out the dress code and decide what to wear. Formulate a few interesting questions in your mind and rehearse these so that you are not stuck for words when you get to the networking event.

Hot Tip

Carry business cards with you EVERYWHERE (yes, have some made up with your contact details on). It is amazing who you might meet and want to exchange cards with.

During the event

Get to the networking meeting ahead of time; this will give you more chance to network before the event officially starts. If you are there first it puts you in a strong position because you can meet people as they arrive and introduce them to others you have already met.

Who to talk to

Take a deep breath and walk tall, you are as good as anyone else there. If you recognise someone you know that's great otherwise you could head for the tea & coffee or food table as these are great places to start up a conversation.

Have the confidence to join already formed groups, it is your right to go and talk to people and you are, after all, at a networking event. However, just have a think about the type of groups to join. Try ONE person stood on their own – join them, they will be your friend for life (or at least for the duration of the event). Or THREE people stood together but at 90 degrees to each other. This configuration creates an open space, a 'welcome mat', for a visitor. Go join them and talk in the group or in a pair.

Figure 39 Join someone on their own (Gatsby 1, 4)

Figure 40 Join an 'open' three (Gatsby 1, 4)

What to say to other people

When meeting someone, keep a hand free to shake hands, a firm handshake is a good start. At the same time, SMILE and MAKE EYE CONTACT.

Introduce yourself then listen carefully for the person's name and repeat it back to them. If it's an unusual name, ask them where it comes from. Then ask about their business and look interested!

Hot Tip

Roger Ailes said: 'we only get 7 seconds to make an impression' and, we don't get a second chance at making the right first impression. Other studies by Nalini Ambadi and Alexander Todorov showed that we form an opinion of others in as little as one tenth of a second. Just be yourself and make a positive impression – you know you can do it!

Hot Tip

To help you with questioning you could formulate a list of question themes (work, holidays, travel etc), put these into pictures in your mind and then link them together in a stack. Using this memory technique will overcome the embarrassing pauses we sometimes get during conversations.

Consider your questioning style: Always try to ask OPEN questions that require an answer which is more than Yes or No. An open question might be: what do you think about ...? or, what would happen if ...? These questions keep the conversation flowing and are preferable to CLOSED questions such as: did you have a good holiday? Or is business good at the moment? These closed questions can result in Yes/No answers and can, therefore, stifle the conversation.

Listening

People love to talk about themselves so learn to LISTEN (we have two ears and two eyes and only one mouth, so we should try and converse in that ratio). Make every effort to turn the conversation back to them.

E.g.: keep your story short – I went to Spain, it was great. Where did you go for your holidays?... and keep the questions coming! Be sincere as insincerity can be spotted a mile off.

L I K E	Their Name	
	(house)	
	(family)	
	(roadworks sign)	
	(bowling)	
K N O W	?	What Why When Where How Who
	(mug)	Date:_____ Time: _____ Place:_____

Figure 41 Interaction checklist (Gatsby 1, 4)

You could use an interaction checklist as shown in Figure 41 to help you remember the questions to ask people.

Hot Tip

Remember to ask for the other person's business card and give them yours. Never, ever, force your business card on anyone. As soon as you can, and discretely, make a note on their Business card to remind you where and when you met them (this will be useful later).

Your values, your brand and your USP

As well as being pleasant and personable, the secret of networking is to have some kind of differentiation. Have a think about your Unique Selling Point (USP), features which enable you to do things better, faster or cheaper than others' in your sector. You need to be aware of your values and what makes you, and your offering, special. It is best to start thinking of yourself as a 'brand' (like Coca Cola, Nike or Hewlett Packard).

Elevator Pitch

At some networking events you may be asked to introduce yourself and talk about your business. You therefore need to have an Elevator Pitch up your sleeve so you could consider putting one together. This is where you talk about yourself, your business and, most importantly, the benefits of doing business with you, in around one minute. You could construct your elevator pitch using the AIDA framework (Attention, Interest, Desire, Action) as introduced in the section on Pitching and Presenting.

Moving on (called 'working the room')

Depending on where you are and who you meet, you will probably want to move on to meet more people.

Be careful not to offend someone by leaving them too soon, and try not to stay in a conversation too long. If you don't believe there will ever be any synergy with the other person then continue to 'work the room'. At the end of the event remember to say GOODBYE to your host/hostess and to anyone you have spent some time with.

After the Event

A networking meeting is just the 'tip of the relationship iceberg'. In order to form useful, lasting relationships, it is <u>critical</u> that you follow up after the networking event. Go through all the Business cards and respond to most contacts, politely, and in a timely fashion.

<u>Exceed Expectations</u>

You may have been asked for some information or you may have promised to follow up on a specific point. Ask your contact for a few days to allow you to get back to them and then exceed their expectations by getting back to them immediately if possible. NEVER find yourself in a situation where your new contacts are chasing you.

Hot Tip

You are now in control of the situation. This is why it was important to take their business card from them. You are much more likely to get a response or follow-up meeting by phoning than by sending an e-mail. Then, when you phone your contact refer to your meeting/conversation at the event to refresh their memory. Always be confident and positive when you phone and keep a smile on your face as this gesture is transmitted over the airwaves.

<u>The answer is almost, always, YES</u>

If, after a network meeting, people ask to meet you, then find the time for a coffee, you never know when you will need them and they will really appreciate your support. You do not know what they will be doing next and who it might lead you to in the future.

Hot Tip

Continue to keep in touch. When driving around, drinking tea or just when you have a spare few minutes, think about people you have not contacted for a long time and give them a call. You are just touching base to check they are ok and it may result in a meeting. They will also think highly of you for thinking of them.

<u>Is it working?</u>

And finally, monitor your progress. Ask yourself questions like: How is networking working for me?, Am I attending the right events? Am I meeting the right people? What do I need to be doing differently? Try out different networking groups and find the ones that work for you.

<u>How to find people</u>

Contacts can be found through various groups such as: Alumni, BNI, 4Networking, Forward Ladies, Chambers of Commerce etc. You just need to try a few and pick the right one(s) for you. You can also find contacts online through sites such as: LinkedIn, Facebook, Twitter, etc.

Hot Tip

You can boost your networking opportunities by contributing to others' blogs and commenting on articles in a really constructive way. You will then be viewed as a 'contributor'.

Finally

Try to think of networking as, at least, a four-touch relationship process. Something along the lines of: Meet – Like – Know - Trust.

Never ask people for job opportunities or for their business during the early stages of this relationship model. Eventually, after a few meetings you can ask people for their help in finding a job, putting you in contact with decision makers or talking about doing business together. You will know when the time is right and, if you don't ask you may never know what opportunity you have missed.

Hot Tip

PEOPLE TALK so make sure they are only saying positive things about you when you are not there! You never know what a contact knows or more importantly who they know, so treat each person as if they were your next biggest client.

Let's go networking, it gets easier with practice!

Interpersonal skills and relationship building – people buy from people so make sure you are friendly, approachable and helpful. Try to see things from the other person's point of view and be genuinely interested in their activities. Try and find out more about them as they may be able to put you in contact with an employer.

There is a well-known interaction model called 'The Six-degrees of Separation' and it states that we are all connected to a person, who might be able to help us, within 5 contacts. It was originally set out by Frigyes Karinthy in 1929 and made more popular by Stanley Milgram who ran an experiment in the 1960's. Milgram arranged for 160 separate letters to be sent (and signed for) from Omaha, Nebraska to a Stockbroker in Sharon, Massachusetts. It transpired that the letters did not follow parallel paths but, instead, the flow was pyramidical. Indeed, all letters that arrived with the Stockbroker went through the hands of three of his associates; Jones, Brown and Jacobs. Milgram then concluded that we can reach a person we wish to speak with via a maximum of 5 connections.

Pyramids and Connectors

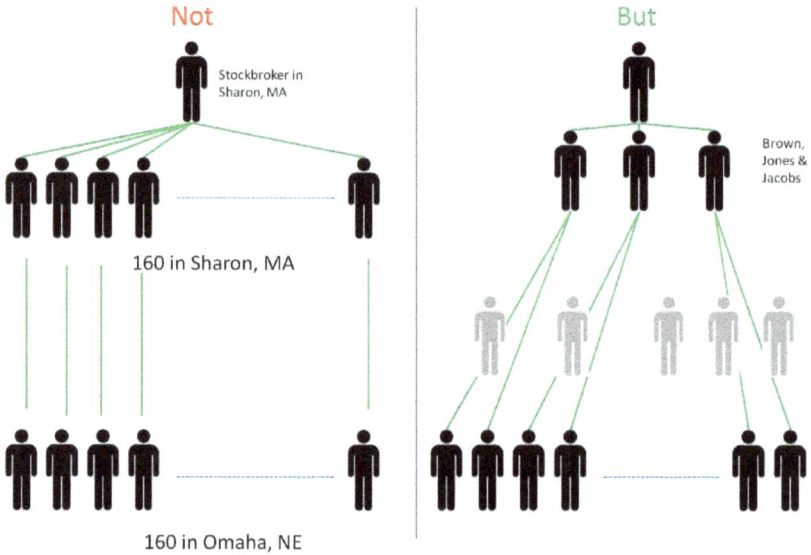

Figure 42 Pyramids and Connectors – 6-degrees of separation (Gatsby 1, 4)

Therefore, it might be worth having a think about the people in your network and identifying people who can connect you with a potential employer. Take a look at the chart in Figure 43 as a starting point. The 6 degrees of separation means that you have access to over 600,000 people (not that you need so many).

Try to think of a few people in each of the categories in Figure 43 who might be able to introduce you to decision-makers in the workplace.

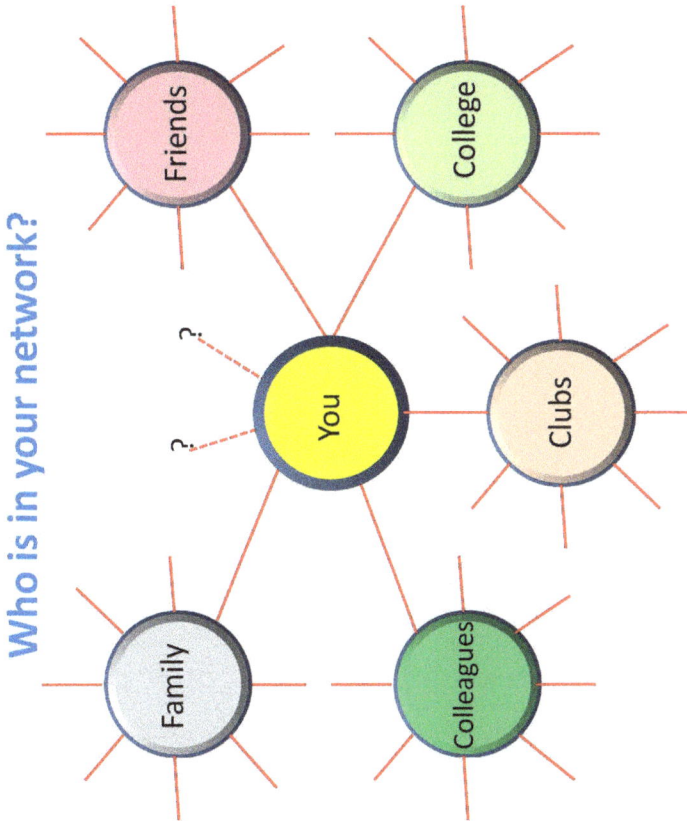

Figure 43 Who is in your network? (Gatsby 1, 4)

Please find, in figures 44 and 45 some handy networking tips

Figure 44 Handy Networking Tips part (Gatsby 1, 4)

Ask for their business card

Write: venue, date and interesting fact on the back.

Always follow up

The event is just the tip of the iceberg. Ask permission to call.

Smile when you call your contacts

Follow up and go for coffee. Monitor your progress.

Use physical and social networks

Twitter, Facebook, LinkedIn etc.

Be Yourself

Enjoy the experience.

Develop yourself.

Don't try to sell yourself.

Give, give, give

Be useful to others. Give people a reason to talk about you.

Networking is a relationship building process

Be patient. Meet - like - know - trust.

"Changing attitudes...

ATTITUDE

... for business success"

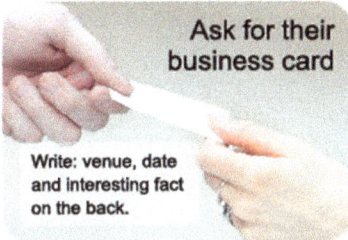

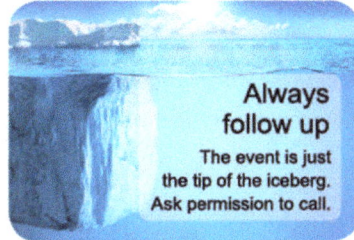

Figure 45 Handy Networking Tips part 2 (Gatsby 1, 4)

How to Work in a Team

Most prospective employers would probably want you to work in a team so here are some simple rules about teamwork.

Not everyone is a natural when it comes to working in a team. However, teamwork is one of the vital ingredients in most forms of employment and without it companies tend to struggle.

Even if the role you seek seems highly independent and you perform most of it remotely or alone, you will still need to communicate with others about your tasks, and understand what others are doing in the context of the organisation where you will work.

Because of this, interviewers almost always test whether you have teamwork skills - and if you demonstrate a lack of these, or no such skills at all, you are unlikely to be successful at interview. Employers need people who can get along with each other.

What do Employers understand by teamwork?

Employers view teamwork as the ability to work amicably with fellow employees in all kinds of situations and with empathy and mutual respect and understanding. Teamwork requires individuals to not only have people skills but also a sense of maturity, which allows the individual not to get upset over trivial matters.

Teamwork involves supporting and encouraging other members of your team to achieve a common goal quickly and effectively. Team members can also be leaders or followers so, in an interview, you can use an example of where you have led a team or followed someone else towards your shared vision. Being a leader within a team, though, is one of the competencies employers are most interested in.

Why Are Teamwork Skills So Highly Valued?

Mainly because teamwork skills have a double benefit: a harmonious workplace environment plus more effective work. Teams that gel well are far more likely to impress clients, complete projects and win business. The reputation of a company often rests on how effective its teams are.

Types of Teamwork Skills

Teamwork involves a wide range of skills and, here are five different skill areas that are important for a good team player.

Communication Skills in a team

Team members need to be able to communicate both verbally and by the use of body language, on both emotional and intellectual levels, in a professional manner. Effective communicators:

- Are able to explain their ideas clearly
- Listen to others carefully and with genuine interest
- Make efforts to express their feelings without sounding threatening
- Try to sense or understand how others feel, based on what they are saying and by their body language
- Ask questions whenever they want clarification or are uncertain about something
- Often reflect on events and interactions that took place, how things could have gone better and how things might be different in the future.

Avoid creating undue tension between others, and try to resolve tension rather than build on it

Support Skills

Team members can show support for one another in a number of ways, including congratulating others on their achievement, or empathising in more challenging times. A key element of support is the ability to respect each another in a team.

Problem-Solving Skills

Certain problem-solving skills entail a level of experience and expertise, whereas others are based on analytical competency. Problem-solving skills are concerned with the capacity to assess a given situation and arrive at a positive solution. In a team environment, problem-solving skills are highly valued because employees are expected to develop solutions, together as a team, to situations that may otherwise get out of control.

Listening and Feedback Skills

To ensure proper feedback is given in the various situations arising in a team it is important to listen actively (or generatively). Clarifying what other team members mean, and taking a genuine interest in their problems, demonstrates that you care about them and their development. Feedback is best delivered on a face-to-face basis as this is more personal and interactive.

Conflict Management Skills

Conflict in the workplace is something many of us experience at some stage. How you deal with conflicts can make a big difference to your career. We should try not to let our anger or frustration get the best of us. Ultimately we should try to reach a solution that benefits the team overall.

Teamwork Competency Questions

Interview questions on the subject of teamwork will vary depending on the competency that the interviewer is asking you to demonstrate, but for questions surrounding teamwork you might wish to use the STAR technique as described in the chapter on interviewing.

Sample questions may include:

What is your definition of a good team player?

Do you consider yourself a good team player? Why or why not?

Describe a situation where you were successful in getting people to work together effectively.

How to answer Teamwork Questions

When answering teamwork questions, try to relate your answers to real situations that you have experienced.

Thinking about timing

In an interview situation, some interviewees tend to either drag out their answers, or make their responses too short due to being nervous and, as a result, they miss out on key points relating to their answer. As a general rule try to make your answers between two and five minutes long and include only the most relevant information about your ability to work successfully in a team.

Situation

Try to make sure the example situation that you cite is as unique and relevant as possible. The best scenarios include positions where you led a team, listened to other team members and used their information and feedback to help develop your own situation. This will demonstrate that you can not only work effectively in a team, but also that you are willing to listen to the feedback of others to improve your own approach.

Another useful scenario to mention is one where you resolved conflict with another team member. Ideally this will show how you handled this professionally without letting your emotions get in the way, and without having to escalate this to a higher authority to have the matter resolved for you.

Hobbies and interests

Many examples you could use in answering teamwork questions will be from your activities outside of work. For example, sports such as football or rugby demand teamwork and vigilance. Besides this, mentioning hobbies is useful to demonstrate to the interviewer that you are not solely focused on work and that you have other interests.

Understanding difference

We are all different, unique and special so the person interviewing us, and the people in the team we may ultimately work in, might be different from us but that does not make it wrong. Therefore, please spend a little bit of time getting used to people who may not have the same values and drivers as us. One of these people may just be your future boss.

Team-working skills can be mastered by all kinds of people, from many different backgrounds, although some take longer than others to master these skills. Teamwork skills are continuously being developed and they can be improved and fine-tuned with experience.

Managing your Time and Maximising your Opportunities

Job hunting can be quite time-consuming so make sure you know how best to approach this.

Recognising that "You can't manage time; but you can manage your activities within a time frame", so the focus should be placed on analysing the working day and planning an active time management strategy.

In this chapter we will explore some established tools to aid the analysis and resolution of time conflict. We will focus on the task-specific elements of the job but will not ignore the integration, and emotional aspects, of daily life.

We will look at stress management and the use of decision making and problem solving strategies. This is designed to help busy people plan and organise their day so that they are more productive and have significantly less stress in their lives. This chapter provides Time and Life Management Skills in order to add value to you and your prospective employer.

Each day we are granted 24 Hours or 1440 Minutes or 86,400 Seconds. Ordinarily, this time is divided into three segments; work, play and sleep as shown in Figure 46. When we are on the lookout for work it is important that we balance these segments such that we spend sufficient energy on the career search but we also enjoy some 'play' time in order to refresh our minds. The icing on the cake then, is to maximise our sleep patterns such that we end up with, not just Time Management, but Total Life Management as shown in Figure 47.

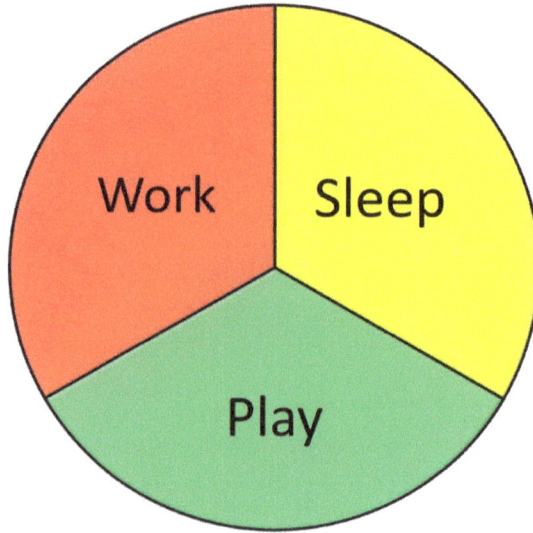

Figure 46 Daily time segments (Gatsby 1, 4)

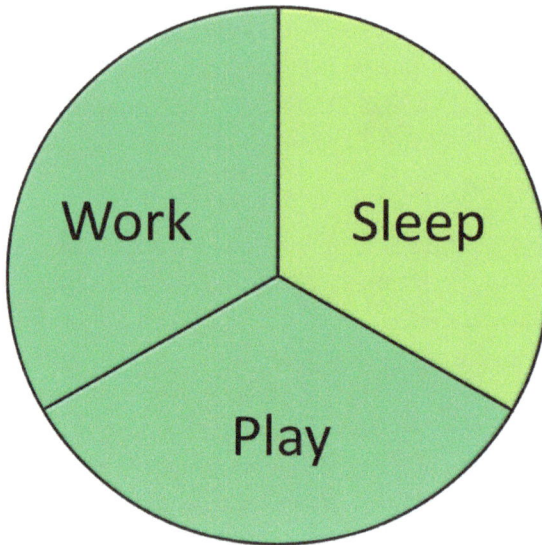

Figure 47 Total Life Management (Gatsby 1, 4)

Where does our time go?

Exercise:

When we are embroiled in a career search, we have many things going on in our head. Therefore, it is worth taking some time to think about what is currently being stored in our brain.

Write down all the things, in your head, that you need to do in the near future and categorise them in to home, work, social, etc.

Example: complete CV, go to Gym, submit application form, take the dog to the grooming appointment, make some phone calls, go to the supermarket etc

_____

_____

_____

_____

- -

Now, pick one to do by tomorrow, delegate one, delete one and date one.

*ASAP means **A**lways **S**chedule **A** **P**recise date and time.*

Tomorrow: _____

Delegate: _____

Delete: _____

Date: _____

When you are looking for work, it is important to remember that your time takes priority. So who is stealing **YOUR** time **from YOU**? Write down a list of suspects (friends, colleagues, neighbours, cold callers etc).

_____

_____

Now, determine what your biggest personal challenge regarding Time Management is?

_____

_____

Focus on a goal, raise awareness and take responsibility. What one thing are you not doing right now that if you were to do on a regular basis, would make a tremendous positive difference to your life and work search?

_____

_____

What is your **Personal Objective** in respect of managing your time?

SPECIFIC, MEASURABLE, ACHIEVABLE, REALISTIC, TIME BOUND.

Objective _____

Specifics _____

Measure (s) _____

How Achievable _____

Realistic _____

Time bound _____

Are you BUSY or PRODUCTIVE?

1. What is the difference between being **BUSY** and being **PRODUCTIVE**?

_____

How can we move from the BUSY state to the PRODUCTIVE state?

_____

We've always done it that way!!! How can you move from being efficient to being effective?

2. Efficient v Effective

_____

3. Distractions and Interruptions

Just when we thought it was going to plan – consider the many interruption opportunities, and the nested levels of interruption. What are the distractions in <u>your</u> working life, preventing you from being productive?

_____

_____

How can you manage these distractions and interruptions?

_____

_____

4. Pareto knew how to manage time (the 80/20 rule)

80% of results come from 20% of efforts
80% of activity will require 20% of resources
80% of the difficulty in achieving something lies in 20% of the

challenge etc.

How to manage yourself in time

Eisenhower and then Stephen Covey used quadrants to represent categories of activities to help manage time based on URGENT and IMPORTANT dimensions. Important and Urgent can then be seen as **two dimensions** on a matrix as shown in Figure 48.

Important embraces your mission, roles and goals.

Urgent embraces things which are pressing upon you, like a ringing phone (which might just be a total waste of time). This has no attachment to your roles and goals but it wants to be answered and it is easy to get sidetracked.

Quadrant 1 – problems and crises that need to be attended to or you don't survive, like important meetings etc.

Quadrant 2 - attaches to your mission, roles and goals but there is not a sense of 'now' about it.

Quadrant 3 - it's pressing, like a ringing phone or unanswered email. Distracting things which might be important to other people, but not always helpful to your mission or that of the organisation.

Quadrant 4 – time-wasting, pleasant things like playing Solitaire, unnecessary meetings, unprepared meetings, etc. Being BUSY but accomplishing nothing.

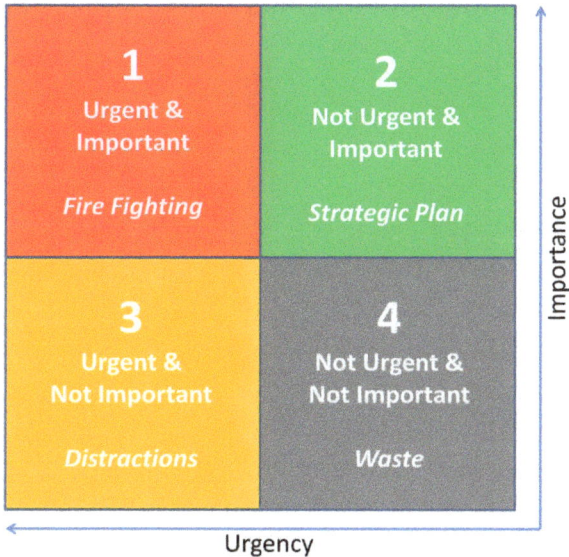

Figure 48 Time Management Quadrants (Gatsby 1, 4)

<u>Exercise:</u> Now populate the quadrants, in Figure 49, with examples in your life. E.g. phone is ringing, project deadlines, planning, Social Media etc.

1 Urgent and Important	2 Not Urgent and Important
3 Urgent & Not Important	4 Not Urgent & Not Important

Figure 49 My time in quadrants (Gatsby 1, 4)

Here is a simple exercise to help you maximise your time.

Q1. Recap one thing could you do (you are not doing now) that if you did on a regular basis, would make a tremendous positive difference to your career planning?

_____

Q2. What one thing would bring similar results to your life generally?

_____

Q3. Now which quadrant would you put those two things in?

Would it be Q2? Because it is important but not urgent. Were it important, you would be doing it now and consistently.

 If you neglect Q2, then Q1 gets bigger (prevention is better than cure). The Q1 activities may consume your life, resulting in management by crisis and robbing you of your energy.

If you attend to Q2, then Q1 gets smaller, reducing fire fighting.

To get the time and attention to work on Q2 activities, you need to do less in Q3 and Q4. In fact, Q4 is totally worthless.

Even activities outside of your career focus (like leisure) are important and therefore belong to Q2.

Q3 also has lower value to you (even though it may be important to other people, it does not help you progress and do your job well). Always work on things that matter most and you will get your time back. **This does not mean that you should not help others!**

Work on Q2 activities to reduce Q's 1, 3 and 4.

Personal development, organising, planning, exercise, education etc., all belong to quadrant 2.

Some hints and tips to help you manage your time

Do only what you can

Clear your clutter

Do less of what drains you & more of what boosts you

Get some support

Keep a To-Do List

Set Personal Goals

Prioritise

Manage Distractions

Avoid Procrastination

Take on the right amount of work (learn how to say no)

Don't Thrive on 'Busy'

Avoid Multitasking

Take Breaks

Scheduling Tasks effectively

Social Media Management

E-mail management – templates, rules, specified time slots etc.

Customer Relationship Management (CRM) – systems to organise, track and keep your contacts informed

Expectation management

Mobile Apps

What other time management actions can you take?

To meet or not to meet

How much time do you spend in meetings? Ask yourself, Do we need to meet?

A few years ago, a leading technology company saw its profitability and productivity declining. It surveyed 30,000 employees worldwide and respondents claimed that only 54% of meeting time was well spent. There is also a ripple effect that these meetings have on the organisation.

But meetings don't have to get the best of you. You can:

Have a purpose
If you don't know why you're meeting, don't meet! Before calling a meeting, think about whether you could inform people through a different medium, or use a tool to reach a decision.

Manage the invitation list
In many companies, it's bad form not to invite lots of people to a meeting. What people don't realise is that every additional attendee adds cost and gets in the way. Remember the '**Rule of 7**': every attendee over a total of 7 reduces the likelihood of making a good, quick, executable decision by 10%. When you have 16 or 17 people, your potential for decision effectiveness is close to zero.

Change the default time. Not too long ago, most companies called 30-minute meetings. Now the typical default time has grown to one hour.

If you do need to meet, consider the protocols for effectiveness:

1. All meetings must have a concrete, measurable goal.
2. All meetings must have a "focusing agenda."
3. No meetings are to be longer than one hour.
4. All background is to be available, at least, the day before.
5. Latecomers will not be briefed on what's been said.
6. Discourage smartphones/tablets unless this is pre-agreed.
7. There will be no formal presentations.
8. Meeting results will be documented and distributed.
9. Follow up

Effective delegation

Job searching is time consuming and we may be continuing to perform tasks that someone else could do for us which, in turn, would free up some of our time. We sometimes hold on to tasks because we are emotionally connected ('our baby') or we do not believe that others' would perform the task in the same way that we are used to.

You should delegate when the task:
– Is not your strength and someone else has more skill
– Requires a lower (higher) level of expertise
– Will take more time than you have and someone else has the time
– Would be a good training opportunity

To delegate effectively it is useful to clearly write down the following:

1. Identify the task
2. Determine:
a) Who has the skill, ability and time, OR
b) Who is ready to be trained on this task

Delegation Steps

1. Explain why the job is important.
a) How does it fit with the team goals?
b) How does it contribute to your organisation's success?

2. Describe how to do the task and what is needed in terms of outcomes.
a) Invest time and write the required outcomes down.
b) Write the outcomes as a SMART goal.

3. Give the person the authority they need to do the job.
a) Allow them to contribute their own ideas on how to proceed.
b) Make sure others know that you have given this person the authority.

4. Indicate when the job needs to be completed and reach agreement.

5. Check for understanding by asking the other person to:
a) Summarise their understanding of the task, expected outcomes, checkpoints and deadlines.
b) Encourage the person to ask questions.

After Delegating:

1. Follow-up at checkpoints / milestones.
2. Give positive and constructive feedback.
3. Make yourself available for interim consultation.
4. Accept risk—avoid perfectionism.
5. Limit standards to what is acceptable and expect a learning curve.

Delegation Preparation Activity

Identify a task to be delegated _____

Why is this job important? _____

Identify someone who would benefit from learning new tasks through delegation. Select a person you identified and prepare to practice delegating the new task. Use the space below to make preparations.

Name:_____

How do you do the task? What outcomes do you want? (Write it as a SMART Goal)

What authority or materials will the person need to complete the task?

 When does the task need to be completed?

When will you check back with them to assess progress?

Keeping a track of time

Time Management Activity Record (Managing time by scheduling and protecting my key activities)						
	Mon	Tue	Wed	Thu	Fri	Comments (follow up)
am						
Lunch						
pm						

Figure 50 Daily time recording sheet (Gatsby 1, 4)

Your can keep a track of your daily activities by using a template, similar to Figure 50, to record events.

Procrastination

Many people procrastinate and put things off from time to time. Sometimes it's those small things – like sorting through mountains of paperwork or tidying your sock drawer. But sometimes it's the bigger things that require more time, more commitment, and might carry more risk of failure in our important job search. This could include freshening-up our CV, making that call to a decision maker or daring to go out to a business networking event.

We might be tempted to come up with a number of reasons why 'it just isn't the right time' or I am too busy or something else that gets in the way of carrying out the tasks that matter. We often find excuses for not taking control of important tasks because it might push us out of our comfort zone and might upset our emotional state.

Our fear of taking charge makes us hang on to the hope that if we procrastinate long enough, our situation will improve. We might convince ourselves that 'one day', perhaps tomorrow, we will be ready to make a change.

However, as time goes by, our fears grow larger, not smaller, until they eventually cause us some harm. By choosing to put off today what can be done tomorrow, we might impact our happiness, confidence and future plans.

A few hints and tips to help with procrastination

1. As we mentioned earlier, **write down your SMART goal and give yourself a deadline** - A goal, or an action item, without a deadline can be put off for ever.

2. **Break your goal into small pieces -** The bigger your goal or the change you want to make, the more quickly it can send you into overwhelm. So if your goal feels daunting, break it into manageable, bite-sized chunks or milestones. You don't have to have every step mapped-out, just the next few steps

immediately ahead of you.

3. **Visualise the future you want** - Picture yourself in a favourite place celebrating what you've accomplished. Imagine your friends and family celebrating your success with you.

4. **Feel the fear** – Yes, job searching is a busy and demanding time and it might put you under a bit of pressure. Just be prepared to feel the fear and accept that it will go away if you approach your career search with a positive mindset.

5. **Build a support network** - Enlist a group of people (selected friends, colleagues and family) who will become your support team. Agree a regular time to meet and let them know how they can help you.

6. **Reward yourself** –Establish a reward system to make sure you celebrate progress and small successes along your journey. This could be having fun with friends or a personal treat. Just make sure you do something to acknowledge your progress, effort and determination.

7. **Create quick wins and build momentum** – When you have your career selection plan, try to have some quick wins (like securing a few interviews or completing a social media campaign). This will build early confidence for you. Then, as you continue, build momentum, lay a trail of concrete leads and keep pushing out of your comfort zone – this is where the personal growth is. With this approach, one day you are likely to land that dream role.

E-mail Management

E-mails are really useful for keeping in touch with prospective employers, recruitment agents and other contacts involved in the job search process.

Many of us feel overwhelmed by email and, although it's a great communication tool, people often overuse it. When managed effectively, though, you can significantly boost your career search productivity. To gain control of your inbox, start by checking and processing email only at certain times during the day. If you're concerned about the delayed response, let people know that you don't check your email constantly (if your Service allows).

But, ... Also, try to keep your inbox as clear as possible.

Organise mail using folders like "Action," "Waiting," and "Archives," And when you do check mail, use the **two minute rule** – immediately handle any email that you can read and responded to in two minutes or less. But, ... What else do you have to manage?

You can also reduce your incoming mail by asking people to send you less.

Try using **Rules**, in Microsoft Outlook, to automate your e-mail.

Stress – what is it and how can we manage it?

In the previous chapter we talked about reaching a situation where we have 'total life management'. In order to get there we should also consider another aspect, that of Stress Management.

Not managing our activities in our time frame can lead to stress, and *"Every sixty seconds you spend angry, upset or mad, is a full minute of happiness you'll never get back!"*

The Stress Management Society defines stress as: "a situation where demands on a person exceed that person's resources or ability to cope". Over 105 million days are lost to stress each year– costing UK employers £1.24 billion. Personnel Today - 700 senior HR practitioners and almost 2,000 employees.

Other findings:

 11% of absence is attributed to stress
 52% say stress is increasing
 60% claim stress is damaging staff retention
 83% think stress is harming productivity

Pressure itself is not bad. But, when those pressures exceed a person's ability to cope, that is when the problems start. We can tackle stress either by reducing pressures or by increasing coping resources – or a combination of the two.

Stress is caused by two things.

Primarily it is down to whether you think situations around you are worthy of anxiety. And then it's down to how your body reacts to your thought processes.

This instinctive stress response to unexpected events is termed *fight or flight'.*

What is stress?

When an organism experiences a shock or perceives a threat, it quickly releases hormones that help it to survive (Walter Cannon 1932). In humans these hormones help us to run faster and fight harder. They increase heart rate and blood pressure, delivering more oxygen and blood sugar to power important muscles.

They increase sweating in an effort to cool these muscles, and help them stay efficient. They divert blood away from the skin to the core of our bodies, reducing blood loss if we are damaged. As well as this, these hormones focus our attention on the threat, to the exclusion of everything else. All of this significantly improves our ability to survive life-threatening events.

Life-threatening events are not the only ones to trigger this reaction. We experience it almost any time we come across something unexpected or something that frustrates our goals. When the threat is small, our response is small and we often do not notice it among the many other distractions of a stressful situation.

Unfortunately, mobilising the body for survival has negative consequences too. We are excitable, anxious, jumpy and irritable. This reduces our ability to work effectively. With trembling and a pounding heart, we can find it difficult to execute precise, controlled skills. Focusing on survival means we make decisions based on the good of ourselves rather than the good of the group. We shut out information from other sources and cannot make balanced decisions. Prolonged stress can have a negative impact on our health.

Some stress is good

Research shows that some stress is good. Stress 'revs up' the body thanks to naturally-occurring, performance-enhancing, chemicals like adrenalin and cortisol. This heightens ability in the short term. But...

there is a limit.

If severe stress is allowed to go unchecked in the longer term, performance will ultimately decline. Not only that, the constant bombardment by stress-related chemicals and stimulation will weaken a person's body. Ultimately that leads to degenerating health. Remember it is physically impossible to be anxious and relaxed at the same time.

Manage your activities within the time allowed, by:

- Living in "day-tight compartments" *(yesterday is history, tomorrow is a mystery, today is a gift, that's why it's called the Present!), and:*
- Learning to relax
- Eating the right food in the right quantities
- Reducing alcohol
- Exercising more (where possible)
- Making a list of issues/goals
- Taking deep breaths
- Stop thinking about stress
- Making a goal map (situation now, obstacles, future view)
- Laughing

Do these sooner rather than later!

What else can/do you do to reduce stress?

Problem Solving

If you view your career search as a problem, there are many tools you could use to help solve problems. A few typical ones are:

Talking to other people

Brainstorming

Mind Mapping

SWOT (Strengths, Weaknesses, Opportunities, Threats) analysis

Organise your data into groups using affinity diagrams e.g. KJ analysis

Appreciative Inquiry

SOAR (Strengths, Opportunities, Aspirations, Results)

Take a look at some of these methods and have a go at solving your problem. Understanding the problem is half the battle.

Notes

_____

_____

Keeping motivated during your job search

It's difficult to know exactly how long your job search process will take. You might land that dream job within a few weeks or, as time passes, the rejections might mount up and your motivation level may just drop.

However, this is just the time when you need to believe in yourself and put in more hard work and systematic approaches than ever. One of the main attributes of successful job searching is self-motivation. Here are a few tips to help you stay positive:

Start as you mean to go on - The first 60 minutes of your day are golden. The thoughts you think and the actions you take during this critical time could affect your performance levels for the rest of the day. Instead of getting up late, set your alarm as if you were going to work, have a shower and take a walk to get some fresh air into your lungs.

Set daily goals - If you don't have anything concrete to work on, you have nothing to focus on and could find yourself achieving very little on that day. Goals will keep your mind focused on the things that are important and keep you feeling positive about your future chances of success. Make your goals SMART and remember to celebrate when you achieve a breakthrough. The act of submitting a couple of job applications is a breakthrough.

Create the right environment - There's a lot to be said for being neat, tidy and well-organised. Make an area in your home where you can manage your job search with a phone, computer and everything else you might find in an office as it will help you stay focused on the target. You might also want to change your environment occasionally by working from a café or hot-desking in a local business centre.

Eat right - Your environment also includes what you consume. Make sure you eat lots of fruit and vegetables, stay away from fatty foods and try to limit your alcohol intake. A healthy body can lead to a healthy mind.

Create a support network - Forming an alliance with other job seekers will help you share experiences, get advice and give you an outlet for your inner feelings. Try to meet with your team at least once a week to share strategies.

Remember the law of averages - The more calls you make, the more networking events you go to and the more applications you make, the greater your chances are of finding the job of your dreams. However, try to resist the urge to 'wholesale-target every recruitment company you find. Tailor your CV for each job and, sooner or later, you'll be successful.

Enjoy the process - Job hunting is a time of transition and change and it can also be a very important time for self-development and self-reflection. Try to use this period to reassess your goals, find out what you really want to do and take this opportunity to make yourself the best you can be.

At every stage of your job search, try and get feedback. If you're not being called for interviews then ask someone to have a look through your CV, covering letters and telephone strategy. If you are getting interviews, but not securing the roles then you should find out what you're doing wrong. You can do this by asking the interviewer for feedback or ask a friend to conduct a mock interview with you and provide candid feedback.

Seven Strategies for staying motivated

1. Value Yourself
You are better than you think!
Wear your hat with pride as you are an expert in your field. Valuing yourself will make you feel more positive about life.

2. Diet and Exercise

Eating the right foods can reduce fatigue. Exercise releases mental and emotional blockages, creates endorphins and can help you sleep.

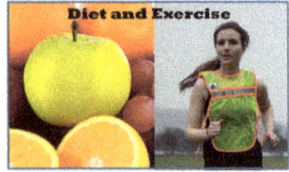

3. Put life in perspective

We might not have a job but we have more than most. Count your blessings to remain positive and motivated.

4. Take control of your mind

Think happy thoughts and see the good in any situation. Attitude is a choice, make the right one.

5. Change your vocabulary and smile

Your emotions and well-being will catch up.

6. Give yourself a daily pep talk

Go through a mental rehearsal of success.

7. Surround yourself with positive people

You are the average of the 5 people you connect with most.

Confirming the job offer

Following the interview/aptitude test phases you might just find yourself receiving a job offer. When the offer comes through, have a good read of the content and make sure the job offered matches the specification you applied against and the role you were interviewed for. It is important to check: the role, the responsibilities in the job, your salary and benefits package and start date.

If all is good, then:

Respond to the employer (or designated contact), in writing, and express your gratitude for the job offer. You've been given an opportunity, and your acceptance letter is the perfect time to show how excited you are to get started. Think about what you're looking forward to the most. Maybe you're on-board with the company's mission, or you're ready to be part of a project you've been told about.

Keep your letter short and sweet, but include these elements:

- A thank-you for the opportunity

- A sentence that says you accept the company's offer of employment

- Your job title

- A recap of the salary and benefits as you understand them

- The date you expect to start

Things to watch out for

So, you have been through the process of looking for a job, you have confirmed the offer and now secured that post of your dreams. This is great and congratulations on your new position. As we start in a new company and begin to get used to our new role and the people in the business, it is worth being mindful that not all new starters stay the course. Sometimes, people leave their employer within a relatively short time of starting (sometimes a matter of months), this is a so-called mis-hire. It is shown * that mis-hires are not due to a lack of competency but mainly due to attitude.

* Hire for Attitude by Mark Murphy CEO Leadership IQ

Why do so many fail within the first 18 months of taking a job?
The research tracked 20,000 new hires, 46% of them failed within 18 months. But even more surprising than the failure rate, was that when new hires failed, 89% of the time it was for attitudinal reasons and only 11% of the time for a lack of skill. The attitudinal deficits that doomed these failed hires included a lack of coachability, low levels of emotional intelligence, motivation and temperament. See Figure 51.

Are technical and soft skills less important than attitude? If so, why?
It's not that technical skills aren't important, but they're much easier to assess (that's why attitude, not skills, is the top predictor of a new hire's success or failure). Virtually every job (from neurosurgeon to engineer to cashier) has tests that can assess technical proficiency, as seen in the earlier chapters. However, what those tests don't assess is attitude; whether a candidate is motivated to learn new skills, think innovatively, cope with failure, assimilate feedback and coaching, collaborate with teammates and so on.

Soft skills are the capabilities that attitude can enhance or undermine. For example, a newly hired team leader may have the intelligence, business experience and financial acumen to fit well in a new role. But if that same person has an authoritarian, hard-driving style, and they're being hired into a social culture where happiness and camaraderie are paramount, that combination is unlikely to work. Additionally, many training programmes have demonstrated success with increasing and improving skills—especially on the technical side. But these same programmes are notoriously weak when it comes to creating attitudinal change.

Technical proficiency, once a guarantee of lifetime employment, is a commodity in today's job market. Attitude is what today's companies are hiring for. Companies want attitudes that perfectly match their unique culture. Google and Apple are both successful organisations, but their cultures are quite different.

The top characteristics of low performers were found to be:

Being negative

Blaming others

Feeling entitled

Not taking initiative

Procrastinating

Resisting change, and

Creating drama for attention.

As the focus on hiring has shifted away from technical proficiency and onto attitude, it has precipitated a lot of tactical changes in how job interviews are conducted. For example, the new kinds of interview questions being asked are providing real information about attitude instead of the vague answers hiring managers used to get.

Savvy employers are less likely to rely on the old standby questions like "tell me about yourself" and "what are your weaknesses?" Companies now have answer keys by which to accurately rate candidate's answers. This is where competency-based and strengths-based approaches come in.

Where are companies finding candidates with the right attitudes? The majority is using social networks but is that even working?

Companies are finding their best people through employee referrals and networking. They also realise that the high performers they already have fit the attitude they want. Moreover, these are the people they should be asking to help find more people just like them.

Given that data, it seems that candidates should be networking in every way possible—including social networking. The chapter on networking gives some helpful hints and tips on this subject.

Attitudes change as workforce dynamics change. What happens in this case?

The attitudes for which organisations should hire are not abstract or based on a theoretical ideal, but rather are just the characteristics that separate high and low performers. High-performing employees live their attitudes every day and it's a big part of what makes the organisations so successful. Low performers struggle with those attitudes and are typically rejected by the culture. Every company has to discover the attitudes that make their organisation unique and special. Even if the company's attitudes change over the years, those attitudes will always be an organic reflection of their most successful people. So, with the right attitude, you can be one of those people.

COACHABILITY – *the ability to accept and implement feedback from bosses, colleagues, customers and others*	26%
EMOTIONAL INTELLIGENCE – *the ability to understand and manage one's own emotions and accurately assess those of others'*	23%
MOTIVATION – *sufficient drive to achieve one's full potential and excel in the job*	17%
TEMPERAMENT – *attitude and personality suited to the job and work environment*	15%
TECHNICAL/ COMPETENCE – *functional skills for the job*	11%

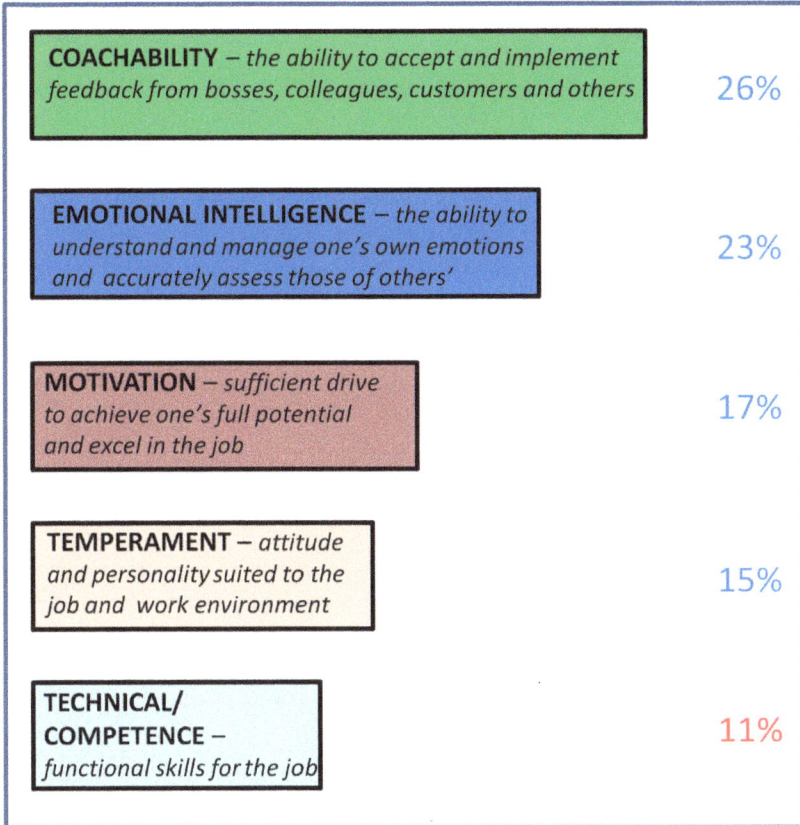

Figure 51 Reasons for mis-hires (Gatsby 1, 4)

Etiquette when in the role

This section maps to Gatsby Benchmarks 1, 3 and 4.

Work etiquette is a code that governs the expectations of social behaviour in a workplace. This code is established to "respect and protect: time, people, and processes". When it comes to work etiquette, there are some rules that we really need to pay attention to. Some of these may seem obvious, but sometimes we could have made a mistake without even noticing it. There is probably no universal agreement on a standard work etiquette, but some guidelines are given below.

1. Greet people
Greeting the people that you come into contact with isn't only polite but it establishes rapport. You never know who the people that you greeted could be, so it is important to greet everyone with the same degree of kindness and politeness.

2. Offer a handshake and make good eye contact
Handshakes are a universal business greeting. Even in the digital age a firm handshake is still considered a positive trait, whereas a weak one gives a negative vibe. It is good to make good eye contact and smile when you shake hands. If you find yourself averting your eyes you might be viewed as lacking social confidence and integrity.

3. Pay attention to names
Names are one of the first pieces of information that we learn about our new work colleagues, work partners, suppliers and customers. It is, of course, how people recognise and address you as well.

4. Adopt Active (or even Generative) Listening
When someone else is speaking, it is important to nod or smile to show to them that you are engaged in the conversation. It helps the other person to recognise that you care about what they say and that you value their opinion. Try not to interrupt the other person and

wait for them to finish talking before you respond.

5. Be polite and professional in all forms of communication
Whether you are meeting face-to-face, over the phone or via email, each, and every, interaction needs to be kept at a professional level.

Earlier in this book we discussed the Mehrabian circle so when you communicate through text only, you don't have the added value of vocal tone or other body language/facial expressions to support the written message. Therefore, try to keep messages short and to the point, and don't transmit anything that you wouldn't say in-person. It is also worth spending a little time to check for grammatical errors as this might really upset certain people. You could use spell checkers on your computer but, bear in mind, that these checkers are not 'sense' checkers.

6. Be Punctual
Whether you are arriving at work, going to a meeting or making a project deadline, punctuality is critical. In business, time is precious and when deadlines are missed, the whole team could be affected and others may have to cover for you. Just make sure that your alarm clock, phone app or other reminders are set up and working and that you check the train/bus times and traffic hold ups.

7. Dress Code
In modern business, dress codes have become much more relaxed. However, just because there is no rule that says you can't come to work in a hoodie, joggers and sandles, it doesn't mean that you should. In work, we are judged on what we say, how we say things and 'how we look'. There is no getting away from it, you will be judged on your appearance so always try to dress appropriately for the sector in which you are working.

8. Hygiene
Irrespective of your company dress code, good personal hygiene must be observed. Always try to have neat hair, keep your beard neatly trimmed, keep fingernails clean and in good condition and make sure

your clothes smell good. People in the workplace are likely to avoid other workers who have body odour or smell of fried food.

9. Manners maketh the man

Whether in the office, factory or company refreshment areas, please make sure that you are polite to others. Also, especially in the dining areas try not to talk with food in your mouth, keep elbows away from the table and try hard (really hard) to keep your phone in your pocket.

10. Phone Etiquette

We live in the digital age where many people have personal phones and other devices. However tempting, when at work we should try and keep our focus on the task in hand and avoid the temptation to be ever glancing at our phones. First of all this can be dangerous. If you accidently fall over, your may injure yourself but your company may also be liable for a health and safety breach. In addition, looking at your phone all day will really irritate your fellow workers and it certainly will not help your concentration levels with the job you have been paid to do.

Observing these simple hints and tips on workplace etiquette could save you a lot of embarrassment and might contribute to you being seen as a model employee. However, we also need to think about the law and consider workplace rules and regulations such as The Equality Act 2010.

The Equality Act 2010

The Equality Act became law in 2010. It covers everyone in Britain and protects people from discrimination, harassment and victimisation. The information below is a snapshot of key points from the Act and is designed to help you understand how to treat people, in your workplace, lawfully and with respect for their preferences.

Who is protected by the Equality Act?

Everyone in Britain is protected by the Equality Act and it protects people against discrimination because of the protected characteristics that we all have. Under the Act, there are nine protected characteristics:

Age

Disability

Gender reassignment

Marriage and civil partnership

Pregnancy and maternity

Race

Religion or belief

Sex

Sexual orientation

There are some important differences depending on which protected characteristic people have. People are protected from discrimination in the workplace but, it is worth remembering that people are protected in the following places:

When using public services like healthcare (for example, visiting your doctor or local hospital) or education (for example, at your school or college)

When using businesses and other organisations that provide services and goods (like shops, restaurants, and cinemas)

When using transport

When people are members of a club or association (for example, your local tennis club)

When people have contact with public bodies like your local council or government departments

People can be discriminated against in four key areas:

Direct discrimination
This means treating one person worse than another person because of a protected characteristic. For example, a promotion comes up at work. The employer believes that people's memories get worse as they get older so doesn't tell one of his older employees about it, because he thinks the employee wouldn't be able to do the job.

Indirect discrimination
This can happen when an organisation puts a rule or a policy or a way of doing things in place which has a worse impact on someone with a protected characteristic than someone without one. For example a local authority is planning to redevelop some of its housing. It decides to hold consultation events in the evening. Many of the female residents complain that they cannot attend these meetings because of childcare responsibilities.

Harassment
This means people cannot be treated in a way that violates their dignity, or creates a hostile, degrading, humiliating or offensive environment. For example a man with Down's syndrome is visiting a pub with friends. The bar staff make derogatory and offensive comments about him, which upset and offend him.

Victimisation
This means people cannot be treated unfairly if taking action under the Equality Act (like making a complaint of discrimination), or if you are supporting someone else who is doing so. For example, an employee makes a complaint of sexual harassment at work and is dismissed as a consequence.

So, when you land that dream job and you enter the workplace, on the first day, please be thoughtful of other people as their preferences could be protected under law.

Support can be found at: www.equalityadvisoryservice.com

The Gatsby Benchmarks

The Gatsby Benchmarks are extremely topical at present having been explicitly referenced throughout the Department for Education's (DfE) Careers Strategy (December 2017) and the later Statutory Guidance for careers (January 2018). They have actually been under consideration since around since 2013.

The Gatsby Benchmarks originated in a research report (Good Career Guidance) from the Gatsby Foundation in 2013. The report was commissioned by Lord Sainsbury and Sir John Holman was appointed to lead a research team to focus on international evidence for 'what works' in career development. The research provides a comprehensive study of career development exploring key elements of good career development, the cost per school (or other educational provision) for good career development and the economic benefit of career development to the economy. Price Waterhouse Cooper were commissioned to provide the latter and summarised that the cost of every NEET individual (people not in education, employment or training) to the government is the same amount required to provide the benchmarks to 280 pupils. The overall annual cost to the government for implementing a good careers guidance strategy is £207 million in the first year and £173 million per year thereafter. The study explored international evidence from The Netherlands, Germany, Hong Kong, Ontario in Canada, Finland and Ireland and the report found 8 benchmarks of best practice, known as 'The Gatsby Benchmarks.' They are shown in the following table:

Benchmark	Description
1. A stable careers programme	Every school and college should have an embedded programme of career education and guidance that is known and understood by pupils, parents, teachers and employers.
2. Learning from career and labour market information	Every pupil, and their parents, should have access to good-quality information about future study options and labour market opportunities. They will need the support of an informed adviser to make best use of available information.
3. Addressing the needs of each pupil	Pupils have different career guidance needs at different stages. Opportunities for advice and support need to be tailored to the needs of each pupil. A school's careers programme should embed equality and diversity considerations throughout.
4. Linking curriculum learning to careers	All teachers should link curriculum learning with careers. For example, STEM subject teachers should highlight the relevance of STEM subjects for a wide range of future career paths.
5. Encounters with employers and employees	Every pupil should have multiple opportunities to learn from employers about work, employment and the skills that are valued in the workplace. This can be through a range of enrichment activities including visiting speakers, mentoring and enterprise schemes.

6. Experiences of workplaces	Every pupil should have first-hand experiences of the workplace through work visits, work shadowing and/or work experience to help their exploration of career opportunities, and expand their networks.
7. Encounters with further and higher education	All pupils should understand the full range of learning opportunities that are available to them. This includes both academic and vocational routes and learning in schools, colleges, universities and in the workplace.
8. Personal guidance	Every pupil should have opportunities for guidance interviews with a careers adviser, who could be internal (a member of school staff) or external, provided they are trained to an appropriate level. These should be available whenever significant study or career choices are being made. They should be expected for all pupils but should be timed to meet their individual needs.

Figure 52 Gatsby Benchmark Descriptions

As can be seen in the table each of the benchmarks have sub-criteria for how they can be achieved. Along with the 8 benchmarks the report makes 10 recommendations for implementing the benchmarks. The Department for Education initially commissioned the Careers and Enterprise Company to support schools to implement benchmark 5 – Encounters with Employers and Employees. In addition to this the Careers and Enterprise Company have set up a local support network in 38 of the 39 national Local Enterprise Partnerships in the form of Enterprise Coordinators and Enterprise Advisers. The Careers and Enterprise Company has also introduced a free tool, 'Compass', for schools to self-assess against the benchmarks. The Department for Education in its Careers Strategy and Statutory guidance states that schools should achieve all 8 benchmarks by 2020. Most schools will meet all of the benchmarks.

At present there is considerable work being done between the Gatsby Foundation and the Quality in Careers Standard to better align their criteria. The Department for Education, in its strategy and statutory guidance, **strongly recommends** that schools use the **Quality in Careers Standard** to externally validate their progress towards the 8 Gatsby Benchmarks.

Focus on engaging with employers and aligning with Gatsby benchmarks 5 to 8

So far, in this book, our references to the Gatsby Benchmarks have been focused on **learning activities** that you can do in order to prepare for the world of work. Whilst it is important to have a good set of skills and a positive mindset towards career development and job searching it is also valuable to you and to a prospective employer if you have some basic knowledge of **'real' workplaces**. To help with this you can follow the guidance in the Gatsby benchmarks 5 to 8 to help you consider building connections with employers and gaining 'first-hand' experience of the workplace.

Gatsby bench-mark	Benchmark Over-view	Actions you could take
5	Encounters with employers and employees – encouraging you to have face to face interactions with the above	Invite employers or employees to engage in any job club or other forum you might belong to. Ask apprentices, ex pupils from school and friends in work if they would like to share their stories of the workplace. Take advantage of Careers Week events by hosting a table and meeting employers.

6	Experiences of Workplaces – arranging workplace visits, work shadowing and/or work experience	Organise a 'walking tour' of local businesses. This takes courage but many employers would be open to showing you their workplace. Create a careers research booklet to keep your employer visit notes in. This is good for reference but also demonstrates your diligence to other employers.
7	Encounters with Further and Higher Education – ensuring that you get to understand the full range of learning opportunities available to you	Make a visit to your local colleges and universities and develop relationships with the people there who can help you with your careers decisions. Make yourself aware of the programmes on offer as you can then share this interest with future employers. Many companies support a dual on-the-job and off-the-job training where you work in the place of employment but also attend college/university on a regular basis. In this way you can learn about the chosen area of study and apply the principles in your new workplace to the benefit of you, your employer and their customers.
8	Personal Guidance – seek out new opportunities for guidance interviews with a career advisor (please see also the links in the 'Useful References and Added Value' table in the following section)	Contact your local careers advice bureau; invite your parents/ guardian along if appropriate. Talk to friends and associates who have received careers advice and find out best practice.

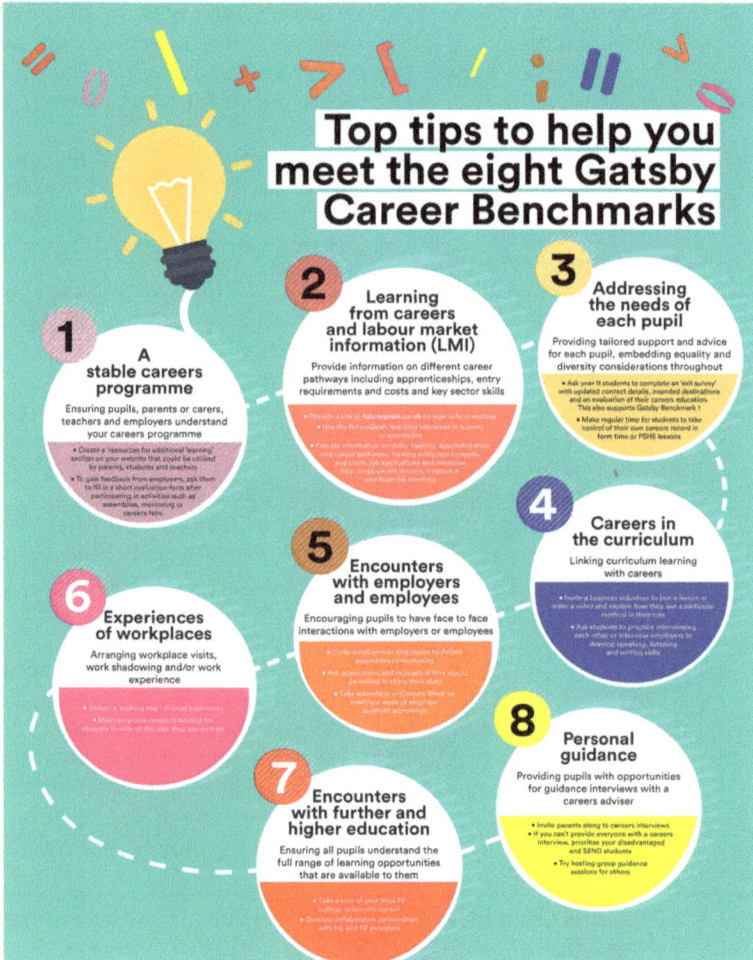

Reproduced by kind permission of Leeds City Region Enterprise Partnership (the LEP)
working in partnership with West Yorkshire Combined Authority

Useful references and Added Value

To help with your job search and career path, some useful weblinks and reference sources that might be of value are shown in figure 53.

Organisation	Activity	Contact
National Careers Service	Provides information, advice and guidance to help you make decisions on learning, training and work.	nationalcareersservice.direct.gov.uk
Job Search	Provides job search directory	www.gov.uk/jobsearch
CV Library	Postcode-selectable open vacancies	www.cv-library.co.uk
Careers online	The website of C&K Careers	ckcareersonline.org.uk
Career Cake	Many resources and video tutorials on job searching	www.careercake.com
Equality Advisory Service	For support with the Equalities Act 2010, workplace etiquette etc	www.equalityadvisory-service.com
The Careers and Enterprise Company	Gatsby Benchmarks	www.careersandenterprise.co.uk/schools-colleges/understand-gatsby-benchmarks

Figure 53 Useful references (Gatsby 3)

Summary

I hope you have enjoyed using this book as a handy, interactive reference guide to your recruitment and career planning. I also hope that it has helped to take the heat out of your job search and assisted you in feeling more positive about moving on to a secure career path.

This book has gone beyond career search and has covered the broader topics of presenting, pitching, confidence, resilience and self-belief. We also looked at the mechanics of career planning, advanced interview skills including coverage of 'strengths-based' and 'competency-based' approaches and networking skills.

I hope you enjoyed the easy-to-read style and trust that this encouraged you to continue browsing and learning more about how to plan and secure an interesting, stimulating, sustainable job.

I trust that the inclusion of the Gatsby references helped you to recognise the core elements of careers advice and hope that the Gatsby cross-referencing was valuable to teachers.

I wish you good luck along your career journey.

Martin Haigh

This book has provided an introduction to the tools and techniques of work readiness, but, for more support and further hints and tips contact: Martin on:

M: +44 (0) 7801 030 004
O: +44 (0) 1484 712 800
E: martin@lattitude7.co.uk
W: www.lattitude7.co.uk
L: http://uk.linkedin.com/in/martinhaigh7
T: @martinhaigh

About the Author

Dr. Martin Haigh MBE is the owner of multi award-winning learning and development business, Lattitude7. He is a Chartered Engineer who holds a Ph.D from Leeds University. Following a career in automotive engineering leadership he became group coach for an international company embracing talent management and organisational development. Martin was responsible for personal development and training for senior leaders from various countries. He also arranges and delivers on international team building seminars.

Martin has been active in management, leadership, presentations and ethics training for many years. He is an NLP Practitioner and an Appreciative Inquiry Practitioner; has been an associate trainer for various organisations, including Leeds University. Martin acquired a business coaching certificate from the Coaching Academy and a business coaching diploma from the Academy of Professional Coaching. He is licenced to deliver accredited training and has a qualification in Cultural Awareness and international interaction.

Martin was an Ethics and Integrity advisor for a Product Development Community in Europe and MEA. A qualified teacher, Martin has a reputation as a highly-effective trainer and, through his international experience and cultural awareness, offers a range of learning experiences to support people, teams and businesses.

He has been helping students with work-related studies for many years and is the Careers Ambassador for Brighouse High School. Martin is also a member of the Enterprise Adviser Network. In his spare time, Martin is a Marathon runner and IRONMAN Triathlete so he knows a thing or two about setting goals and achieving results.

Illustrations and Tables

INDEX

www.ingramcontent.com/pod-product-compliance
Lightning Source LLC
Chambersburg PA
CBHW050820090426
42737CB00022B/3458